Intended for Pleasure

Ed Wheat, M.D. and Gaye Wheat

Intended for Pleasure

Fleming H. Revell Company
Old Tappan, New Jersey

Scripture quotations not otherwise identified are based on the King James Version of the Bible.

Some of the material used in chapters 4 and 11 on basic anatomy and contraception came directly from Dr. Wheat's "Sex Technique and Sex Problems in Marriage" cassettes and appeared by permission in a similar form in *The Act of Marriage* by Tim and Beverly LaHaye, published by the Zondervan Corporation, Grand Rapids, Michigan, 1976.

Material on the P. C. muscles in chapter 6 appears by permission of the Zondervan Corporation.

Appreciation is expressed to Ortho Pharmaceutical Corporation of Raritan, New Jersey, for their gracious permission to incorporate materials from *Understanding Conception and Contraception* into the text of chapters 4 and 11.

Illustrations were adapted from drawings found in a Schering Clinoptikons booklet entitled *Female Pelvic and Obstetrical Anatomy and Male Genitalia*. They are used by permission of the Schering Corporation.

Library of Congress Cataloging in Publication Data

Wheat, Ed.
    Intended for pleasure.

    Bibliography: p.
    Includes index.
    1. Marriage. 2. Sex instruction. 3. Sex in marriage. 4. Family—Biblical teaching.
I. Wheat, Gaye, joint author. II. Title.
HQ734.W52   261.8'34'18   76-52997
ISBN 0-8007-0824-5

TO Ed Wheat, Sr., and Gladys Gibson Wheat, whose commitment, devotion, warmth, generosity, and integrity stood for fifty years as a beautiful picture of genuine agape love.

Contents

Preface

Intended for Pleasure has come about almost unexpectedly; not because I wanted to write a book, but because I had information to communicate which could dramatically change lives, marriages, homes, and families. As a Bible-believing, Bible-teaching family doctor in Springdale, Arkansas, I have found myself these past years becoming more and more involved in marriage counseling because the needs were so great. This has led to speaking and counseling at churches, colleges, seminaries, and other gathering places. Then several years ago came the request from conservative Christian leaders for a teaching cassette series on sex technique and sex problems in marriage which could be used by the Christian world.

As a result of these widely distributed tapes, letters arrive at my office daily from Christians who have heard the cassettes and are anxious to discuss their specific problems with a biblically oriented counselor who has the medical knowledge to help them. The contents of this book have been designed to answer those questions and to meet the needs which appear so frequently in marriage. Both biblical principles and medical solutions to problems of sexual adjustment are discussed in detail with specific instructions for the reader—the kind I would give if he or she were a patient in my own office.

I find that a surprising number of couples are simply missing out on what God intended for them. Some are unhappy and actively seeking answers; others try for contentment while vague longings stir within for the special kind of relationship they have not yet experienced with their marriage partners. Most of these Christian couples have never been taught what the Bible actually says about sex, nor, from the medical standpoint, how to fully enjoy what God has designed for man and wife.

And so this book has been written for every married or soon-to-be-married person who is searching for a medically accurate presentation of sex in marriage within the framework of the Bible's teachings. While the subject matter is discussed quite frankly and with medical precision, it is treated as sacredly and carefully as the Bible itself treats the subject of sex in marriage. The promise of sexual fulfillment is available to any husband and wife who will choose to enter into God's plan for their marriage, and the purpose of this book is to show the way to that fulfillment.

My lovely wife, Gaye, has worked closely with me in counseling, presenting seminars, preparing the cassette series, and now in the writing of this book. Through these pages we want to communicate to every reader our own sense of wonder and joy at what God can do in a marriage when it is committed to Him, with husband and wife possessing both the attitudes and the information necessary for a joyous relationship. We share with you what we ourselves have discovered!

As we begin, please keep one tremendous fact in view: God Himself invented sex for our delight. It was His gift to us—*intended for pleasure*.

ED WHEAT, M.D.
SPRINGDALE, ARKANSAS

Acknowledgments

Gaye and I want to thank many people dear to us who worked as a team to help this busy family doctor and his wife prepare *Intended for Pleasure* for publication. Our deepest appreciation goes to Gloria Okes Perkins, whose writing and editing skills were invaluable to us and crucial to the outcome of this book. We treasure not only her abilities but her Christian love and concern for the needs of others. Many happy hours were spent with Gloria and her wonderful husband, Dan, as we prayed together and worked together on all phases of the manuscript.

We are grateful to Richard and Linda Nilsen, Jerry and Sandi Knode, and Henry Taylor who carefully researched and assembled material for the book; to our daughter, Merry Ann, and to Susan Vanderwater, who lovingly typed and retyped these pages; and to Kayda Grace, M.D., our medical proofreader, who also gave vital assistance in my clinic during this whirlwind of activity. The book could not have been completed had not my nurse-practitioner, Joan McDonald, and my office manager, Alma Beard, spared me from many distractions and worked long additional hours in the clinic, giving our patients extra attention during my times out of the office.

We are particularly appreciative of Martin Bak, who has given untir-ingly of himself in the production of the visual materials. Dale Ellen Beals prepared the medical illustrations with precision, while her hus-band, Benny, graciously taught my men's early morning Bible classes

11

during this busy period. Suggestions offered by our friend Michael
Cocoris of Dallas Seminary were of special help to us. All of these people
have labored together with us in an atmosphere of Christian love which
has drawn us closer than ever before with a warm, mutual respect for the
contribution each has made.

It was a privilege to have my friend of twenty years, LeMon Clark,
M.D., review much of this manuscript. Dr. Clark is truly one of the great
pioneers in the field of sex therapy and his material has been incorporated
into our book in a number of places.

Any recent book on the subject of sex in marriage must draw upon the
significant research done by Dr. William H. Masters and Dr. Virginia
Johnson at the Reproductive Biology Research Foundation in St. Louis,
MO. Today we know far more about the effective treatment of sexual
dysfunction because of their pioneering work in this field. Some of the
practical suggestions in *Intended for Pleasure,* which guide the reader
into sexual fulfillment, reflect the clinical findings of Masters and Johnson
and procedures developed by them.

Our final thanks go to Jody Dillow and Don Meredith of Christian
Family Life, Inc., for their encouragement and assistance in the original
preparation of the sex cassettes which formed the springboard from which
this book has come.

ED AND GAYE WHEAT

Foreword

Dr. Ed Wheat is a much-loved family physician in his own community whose keen interest in helping people has given him a widespread ministry throughout the nation. He is a serious student of the Bible and has taught three adult Bible classes per week for many years. His deep interest in the Word of God is reflected in the strong biblical emphasis given in *Intended for Pleasure*.

During the past few years, modern research has uncovered an amazing amount of information on sexual adjustment in marriage. Unfortunately, most of it is written in such a crass manner that the Christian community has been turned off by it. Dr. Wheat has sifted through this material to present that which is medically helpful in a wholesome manner and with a godly perspective which is sure to have an enriching effect upon the reader.

Some of the material in this book is based on the concepts he first distributed in three-hour cassette form under the title "Sex Technique and Sex Problems in Marriage." I have highly recommended these beneficial cassettes to young people getting married and to married people with unresolved sexual problems. In fact, almost every major Christian-family-life authority in the nation gives a hearty endorsement to his cassette material. Because of the widespread distribution of the cassettes, many have asked that he put his thoughts in written form. The result is this book which I recommend to anyone interested in a wholesome presentation of this very delicate but significant subject.

TIM LAHAYE

PRESIDENT,

CHRISTIAN HERITAGE COLLEGE

AND FAMILY LIFE SEMINARS

13

1

Intended for Pleasure

Scores of people—many of them Christians—come to my office looking for a medical solution to their particular marriage problem. While as an M.D. I can do a great deal to help medically, often there is a greater need for me to first communicate biblical information which can heal wounds, restore relationships, and establish the right foundation for healthy attitudes toward sex in marriage.

Knowing and understanding what God says about any phase of life leads to wholeness in that area; nowhere is this more necessary than in the sexual realm, where negative attitudes have virtually destroyed marriage relationships.

I think of the man who felt deeply disturbed when God and sex were mentioned in the same discussion. To him, sex was altogether separate from his Christian life. The sexual relationship was an unholy activity in his opinion, and yet he continued it with deep guilt feelings which tarnished the experience for both him and his wife. His misconceptions of God's view of sex resulted in a hurried physical act without tenderness or pleasure.

Then I think of the woman who has been married twenty-five years and is still not sure what an orgasm is or whether she has ever experienced one . . . the husband and wife whose egos have been so wounded in the bedroom that they barely speak to one another . . . the earnest Christian couple who have no serious problems but little joy in their sex relationship . . . and many other troubled people whose marriages are filled with misery rather than pleasure.

God has so much to say to all these through His Word! As a Christian physician, it is my privilege to communicate an important message to unhappy couples with wrong attitudes and faulty approaches to sex. The message, in brief, is this: You have God's permission to enjoy sex within your marriage. He invented sex; He thought it up to begin with. You can learn to enjoy it, and, husbands, you can develop a thrilling, happy marriage with "the wife of your youth." If your marriage has been a civil war battlefield or a dreary wasteland instead of a lovers' rendezvous, all that can change. You see, God has a perfect plan for marriage which we may choose to step into at any time, and the mistakes of the past can be dealt with and left behind.

The ancient counsel given by father to son, based upon the wisdom of God in Proverbs 5:18,19, comes across just as clearly to the reader of today: "Let your fountain [your body parts which produce life] be blessed, and rejoice [or ecstatically delight] with the wife of your youth. . . . Let her breasts satisfy you at all times, and be ravished [or filled] always with her love."

It may surprise some of you to learn that the Bible speaks so openly, so joyously of sex in marriage. Almost every book of the Bible has something to say about sex, and Song of Solomon exquisitely depicts the love relationship in marriage. But Genesis, the book of beginnings, shows us most unforgettably what God has always thought about married love.

If we read the first three chapters of Genesis where it is recorded that God created *male* and *female*, we find that "God saw everything that He had made, and, behold, it was *very* good." Interestingly, the creation of light was "good," the creation of land and sea was "good," and, likewise, the creation of vegetation, of fish and birds and animals was also "good." But not until He had created man and woman did God call for our attention with, "Behold, it was *very* good."

With so many "good" things in the Garden and on earth, only one thing was *not good*: "And the Lord God said, It is not good that the man should be alone; I will make an helpmate for him" (Genesis 2:18). In those few words God taught us that for man there is no substitute, no alternative plan, no better companion than his wife. The void which originally was caused by taking "bone of my bone, flesh of my flesh" can be filled only by the presence of woman. Since a part of Adam went to make Eve, a man remains incomplete without his Eve.

God placed almost top priority on sexual union in marriage. We can see in the Genesis account that after God told man not to learn evil by experience (Genesis 2:17), His *second* teaching told man and woman how to relate in marriage: "Therefore shall a man leave his father and his mother, and shall cleave unto his wife; and they shall be one flesh" (Genesis 2:24). God had first divided the woman from the man when He made Eve. But now He commands them to be joined together again as one flesh. In this brief counseling session, even before any sin and its resulting selfishness had entered the human race, we find three basic commands:

> *First*, when we marry, we should stop being dependent on our parents or our in-laws. We are to become completely dependent on our mates to satisfy *all* our needs.
>
> *Second*, the man is the one who is responsible for holding the marriage together by "cleaving" to his wife. *Cleaving* in this sense means to be welded inseparably so that each becomes a part of the other. Therefore, the man is to be totally committed to his one wife.
>
> *Third*, we are commanded to be joined together in sexual union, to be *one flesh*.

The ideal situation God intended for us is shown by the blissful words "they were both naked, the man and his wife, and were not ashamed" (Genesis 2:25). Adam and Eve could see each other as they really were, without shame, disappointment, or frustration. The sex relationship God had designed for them brought the blessings of companionship, unity, and delight—and note that this was some time *before* the command to bear children was given (Genesis 3:16).

God's plan for our pleasure has never changed, and we realize this even more as we consider how we are "fearfully and wonderfully made" (Psalms 139:14). When we discover the many intricate details of our bodies which provide so many intense, wonderful physical sensations for husbands and wives to enjoy together, we can be sure that He intended for us to experience full satisfaction in the marriage relationship.

Some have assumed that the sex act became an unholy practice when sin entered into the world. However, this is ruled out when we see that God's basic counsel on sex in the first chapters of Genesis was repeated by Jesus Christ to the religious leaders of His day: "But from the beginning of the creation God made them male and female. For this cause shall a man leave his father and mother, and cleave to his wife; and they two shall be one flesh. What therefore God hath joined together, let not man put asunder" (Matthew 19:5; Mark 10:6–9). Jesus reemphasized this to His disciples in the next two verses in Mark 10, and again we find these commands reinforced in Ephesians 5:31.

As a matter of fact, the sex relationship in marriage receives such emphasis in the Scriptures that we begin to see it was meant not only to be a wonderful, continuing experience for the husband and wife, but it also was intended to show us something even more wonderful about God and His relationship with us. Ephesians 5:31,32 spells it out: "For this cause shall a man leave his father and mother, and shall be joined unto his wife, and they two shall be one flesh. This is a great mystery, but I speak concerning Christ and the church." *Thus, the properly and lovingly executed and mutually satisfying sexual union is God's way of demonstrating to us a great spiritual truth.* It speaks to us of the greatest love story ever told—of how Jesus Christ gave Himself for us and is intimately involved with and loves the Church (those who believe in Him). In this framework of understanding between two growing Christians, the sexual relationship can become a time of intimate fellowship as well as delight.

This, of course, explains why the marriage union is the only way man and woman can truly enjoy the riches God has planned for them. Because the relationship is specifically designed to illustrate God's unending love for His people, sexual intercourse must be experienced in the context of a permanent, giving commitment. Anything less shortchanges those involved.

Some people have felt uncomfortable about sex because they somehow equate the sexual desire of men with the sexual drive of animals. They should remember that animals breed according to instinct with biological motivation. But man has intercourse as a whole person. He of all creatures is the only one to use reason in choosing to have sexual relations. Husband and wife are the only creatures capable of gaining spiritual unity and a deeper knowledge of each other through the sexual relationship. Let us realize how the bodies of men and women are designed. Even in the sex act itself we are reminded that this is a relationship of persons, not just bodies, for it is no coincidence that man is the *only* creature of God's creation who relates sexually face-to-face.

Scripture suggests that just as we can know God, so we can know our husband or wife in a deeper, higher, more intimate way through the physical act of marriage. *Know* is the term used in the Bible to define our relationship to God; it also is the term used to designate the intimate union of husband and wife. "Adam *knew* Eve" (Genesis 4:1). Mary, speaking of her virginity, said, "How shall this be, seeing I *know* not a man?" (Luke 1:34). Matthew 1:25 says that Joseph *"knew* her not" until after the birth of Christ. The sex relationship offers no more cherished pleasure than this *knowing* of the one you love. With the understanding that our marriage relationship portrays the truths of our relationship with God, we can become free as never before to express our love for our husband or wife fully through the dynamic opportunity of the sex act.

God's viewpoint comes forth vigorously in 1 Corinthians 7:3–5 where the husband and wife are told they actually *defraud* one another when they refuse to give physical pleasure and satisfaction to their mate. The only activity which is to break regular sexual relations is prayer and fasting for some specific cause, and this is to be only by mutual consent for a very limited time.

Although sin did enter the human race in the Garden and brought with it the possibility of perversion of every good thing (including sex), God's plan for His beloved Creation has continued to operate through the provision of the Redeemer, Jesus Christ. By faith people can choose God's way! It is true that our culture is saturated with sex distorted into lust, and desire has been twisted and deformed until it appears as a beast running loose in the streets, destroying God-given boundaries. *Nevertheless our marriage bed is a holy place in the sight of God.* We must be careful to maintain this viewpoint concerning sex in marriage, for it is God's. Hebrews 13:4 says, "Marriage is honorable in all, and the bed undefiled. . . ." We need to treasure and share with our children these positive values God Himself teaches in Scripture concerning the love/sex relationship, always placing sex in marriage in an entirely different light from sex outside of marriage. Sex apart from marriage is spelled out as obvious wrong. Sex in marriage is wonderfully right. Let us never forget it!

I cannot begin to describe the dimensions of the marriage relationship as experienced by the Christian couple who have a total commitment to Jesus Christ, and flowing from that a realization of their own security in spiritual and physical oneness; who have an excitement found only in each other, knowing this is for as long as they live. This genuine, total oneness and completeness somehow cannot be explained to the one who has not yet experienced it. When this kind of relationship exists, many times you will both want to praise our Lord and have communion with Him in prayer, each thanking Him for the other and the complete love you share.

Intended for pleasure—yes, in the fullest meaning of the word. And even then, language does not convey what God has prepared for us!

2

Finding God's Design

Many of you who are seeking sexual fulfillment in your marriage realize that mastery of physical techniques is only part of the answer. Despite the claims of some sex manuals, a couple cannot separate sex from the rest of the marriage, perfecting it and then isolating it, as it were, in an airtight compartment to be used when desired. Everything that happens in a marriage has its effect upon the lovemaking experience.

Because all phases of the biblical plan for marriage must be in operation before we can fully enjoy the sexual union as God designed it, we need to have a clear understanding of His plan. Unfortunately, most of us were not counseled in these matters before we married and so we stumbled through the first few years, at least, trying to find our way to happiness. As a family physician for twenty-five years, I have observed that marriage with its tremendous significance often turns out to be the least-prepared-for event of life. Even as divorce takes on epidemic proportions, young couples continue to venture into marriage remarkably unprepared. Sometimes a brief meeting with the minister before the wedding, then an often elaborate ceremony, and the newlyweds are on their own, to hit or miss in their quest for happiness, while family and friends hope for the best.

I consider premarriage counseling an essential part of my responsibility as a family doctor. It is not only a preventive measure, protecting against family breakups, but it also can trigger a positive course of action which will bring pleasure and joy as the young couple learn to love in an enduring relationship.

The same basic principles which I discuss in premarriage counseling need to be underscored for every reader before we go on to the physical aspects of lovemaking. Although I usually share these with engaged couples, they will undoubtedly be of help to you whether you are a newlywed or celebrating your twenty-eighth wedding anniversary. Actually, very few couples are so advanced in wisdom and years that they could not profit from the following biblical principles.

Since this is almost the equivalent of listening in on a premarriage counseling session in my office, perhaps you would like to know how it takes place. When a couple calls for an appointment for the blood tests which are required by state law, I ask them to listen separately or together to my teaching cassettes on "Sex Techniques and Sex Problems in Marriage." They are to do this *before* they come in for their appointment. These tapes give a clear, thorough presentation of the information every married couple needs for good sexual adjustment, including specific advice for the first few weeks of intercourse. This information can be found in chapter 4, "Understanding the Basics." As the couple listen to the tapes together, he knows what she should do, she knows what he should do, and they both know that they know. Many uncertainties and fears are dispelled, and the couple begin their marriage with an openness of communication in this most intimate part of their life. When they come to my office, they both receive physical examinations, and at that time they ask specific questions based on the information they have received from the tapes. This procedure assures me that they have been told what they need to know, and it affords me the time to go over these basic principles of the God-planned marriage with them during the office call. I generally find that this is the only specific counseling they have received at this turning point in their lives.

For the premarriage counseling session I have prepared a sheet the couple may keep which lists in brief outline eleven biblical principles which help to ensure a happy marriage. Applying these vital principles will improve anyone's marriage, whether that person is a believer in Christ or not. God has set up certain principles by which men are to operate, and these are effective in anyone's life. The only problem is that the non-Christian is unable to implement these principles consistently on a lifelong basis. Only the Christian has within him the person of the Lord Jesus Christ and the Holy Spirit to empower him to carry out what is so clearly specified in the Bible.

Here is the way I discuss these principles point by point with the engaged couple:

1. Reserve funds to allow for a few weeks of uninterrupted time for a honeymoon. "When a man hath taken a new wife, he shall not go to war, neither shall he be charged with any business, but he shall be free at home one year, and shall cheer up his wife whom he hath taken" (Deuteronomy 24:5).

Now in our day we could hardly expect a man to take off for one year. However, there is a definite scriptural principle here. It is that the first few weeks of the marriage are a crucial time for the young couple. To "cheer up" the wife means literally in the Hebrew "to know sexually and understand what is exquisitely pleasing to her" in the physical relationship.

If, like other young people, you are considering spending several thousand dollars for the wedding and a few leftover dollars for an overnight honeymoon, I certainly advise balancing your funds so that you can be free of responsibility for a few weeks while you have time to get to know each other. During that period you will have clearer communication lines than you may ever have again, and if each of you does not come to know the other at the first of your marriage, you will find those communication lines becoming progressively blocked as time goes on.

Never plan on getting married just before entering college or graduate school, when the demand on your time and efforts will be so great. Seminary or medical school, for instance, will require intense concentrated study. So schedule your marriage at the beginning of a vacation time or during a break in employment. Concentrate on each other to establish the right pattern of caring in your marriage.

2. Borrow no money. "Owe no man anything but to love one another" (Romans 13:8). Borrowing money before marriage or soon after is like adding another phrase to the marriage vows: "Till debt do us part." In other words, let not money put asunder what God has put together. A psychology textbook's listing of the most common problems in marriage puts the handling of money at the head of the list. The key factor which creates problems is not how much money but the attitude toward money or the use of money. In fact, in my counseling experience, I have found much more conflict among people with money than those with limited funds.

This advice could be rephrased "Borrow no money to buy depreciating items." Many young couples go deeply into debt to purchase an expensive automobile or a house full of fine furniture. You will be much happier if you buy only what you can afford and then spend your weekends together fixing up your car or building furniture or searching for "treasures" at used furniture sales.

I know one young couple who make a car payment to their savings account each month. When they have enough cash they buy a car, and go on making payments to themselves for the next car. They collect interest instead of paying it out to someone else, and enjoy freedom from debt at the same time. Financial freedom gives you power to utilize your money as you choose, not as the moneylenders choose for you. If you want to enjoy each other and find pleasure in your marriage, do not commit your funds to such an extent that you do not have available cash for the little things that are so much fun to do together.

3. Be independent of in-laws. Leave father and mother. "For this cause shall a man leave his father and mother, and shall be joined unto his wife, and they two shall be one flesh" (Ephesians 5:31). However, *you should not marry without their approval.* "Children, obey your parents in the Lord: for this is right" (Ephesians 6:1).

Before sin entered into the human race two commands were given to Adam. One was not to eat of the tree of the knowledge of good and evil (in other words, not to learn evil by experience). The other command was to get in-laws out of marriage! Looking down the corridors of time at future causes of marriage problems, God said in-laws should not be involved in your marriage. Separating from parents physically, emotionally, and financially is the best possible way to begin a new social unit.

The *man*, by the way, is told to leave his father and his mother and to cleave (to be united totally and inseparably) to his wife—a welding together so that there can be no taking apart. He is commanded to cleave to his wife even before he is told to love her. The Bible does not specify the best age for marriage, but it does establish the principle that the man must be able to be totally independent of his parents and to establish his own home. Statistically, age twenty-six is the best time for a woman to get married and age twenty-seven to thirty-one for a man. That is, fewer divorces result when people marry at these ages. Three out of five teenage marriages now end in divorce.

I encourage you to listen to your parents if they do not want you to marry or if they disapprove of your choice of mate. Not only is this biblical, but remember that your parents know you better than anyone else does. They have the knowledge to discern the qualities you need in a marriage partner, far better perhaps than you do. I suspect that nine out of ten marital problems could be avoided if children would listen to their parents' careful evaluation before they married.

4. *Do not get a TV set for at least one year.* "Ye husbands, dwell with them according to knowledge, giving honor unto the wife. . . . Be ye all of one mind. . ." (1 Peter 3:7,8). This is one of the most surprising things that young people hear from me. It may sound absurd. But did you know that television can be the greatest, most subtle thief of your time? It will steal away those moments that you should be devoting to your mate and, later, to your family. It will take away the most wonderful hours of your day—hours which could be spent in personal communication and sharing, moments when you can best learn to relate to one another. There is no giving, no receiving when you spend your time watching television.

Husband, you are urged to do two things in Scripture: First, study the Scripture; then study your wife. Dwell with her. Be totally at ease together, with full knowledge of each other. This is what marriage is all about.

5. *Never go to bed with unresolved conflict.* "Let not the sun go down upon your wrath" (Ephesians 4:26). "Forgive as Christ forgave" (Colossians 3:13).

The Bible warns us not to harbor anger so that it corrodes into resentment or bitterness. Some people simmer and fume under the surface for days or weeks at a time, but this is not God's way, and it will damage any marriage. Resolve negative attitudes toward each other by the end of the day, or do not go to bed until you do. In every marriage, conflicts arise because two people have come together from different backgrounds, with different educational levels, emotional makeups, desires, and objectives. Conflicts are inevitable. But a conflict becomes a problem only when it is not quickly resolved.

6. *Seek outside spiritual counsel if unable to resolve a conflict within one week.* "Brethren, if a man be overtaken in a fault, ye who are spiritual, restore such an one in the spirit of meekness. . ." (Galatians 6:1). "Follow peace with all men, and holiness, without which no man shall see the Lord . . . looking diligently lest any man fail of the grace of God, lest any root of bitterness springing up trouble you, and by it many be defiled" (Hebrews 12:14, 15) ". . . forgetting those things which are behind. . ." (Philippians 3:13).

The "one week" is a time limit I have suggested. The Bible does not say how soon spiritual counsel is to be sought. But it is important not to let a seed of bitterness take root and grow up to smother your marriage.

7. Seek counsel if the wife is consistently unable to attain good sexual release. "Let the husband render unto the wife her due; and likewise also, the wife unto the husband. The wife hath not power of her own body, but the husband; and likewise also the husband hath not power of his own body, but the wife. Defraud ye not one the other. . ." (1 Corinthians 7:3–5).

We are told in this passage that the husband and wife are actually robbing one another if there is not mutual pleasure in the sexual relationship. The Bible implies that husbands and wives are entitled to certain rights. However, sexual fulfillment is the only one specifically spelled out. God says husband and wife have the right to be sexually satisfied.

If early in your marriage each of you comes to realize how great your responsibility is to fulfill your mate sexually, most problems will be eliminated even before they begin. In almost every case sexual satisfaction can be reached with good counsel, proper information, and an application and practice of the right techniques.

8. Have some Bible study together every day. "Man shall not live by bread alone" (Matthew 4:4). "Let the Word of Christ dwell in you richly" (Colossians 3:15–17). "Cleanse with the washing of water by the Word" (Ephesians 5:26,27). *Accompany this with prayer*: "If any of you lack wisdom, let him ask of God" (James 1:5).

In Ephesians 5:25–28 we read something which is highly applicable to this principle of marriage: "Husbands, love your wives even as Christ also loved the church and gave himself for it, that he might sanctify and cleanse it with the washing of water by the word; that he might present it to himself a glorious church, not having spot or wrinkle, or any such thing; but that it should be holy and without blemish. So ought men to love their wives as their own bodies. . . ."

Christ meets the needs of the Church by washing it and cleansing it with the water of the Word. So ought we to love our wives. It is our responsibility to place before our wives and our families the Word of God.

Husband, as the Word of God is allowed to course through your wife's mind, personality, and very being, she will become the beautiful person God designed her to be. All that would make her less than pure, all that would limit her from becoming a wonderful wife, will gradually be removed as the two of you share in daily Bible study. It is the responsibility of the husband to initiate this. If you don't know how to begin, one way is to listen together to Bible teaching on cassette. Bible Believers Cassettes, Inc., a free-loan library, offers more than a thousand different messages on the subjects of dating, marriage, and the Christian home. (Send fifty cents for catalog: 130 N. Spring St., Springdale, Ark. 72764.) Do have Bible study that is applicable to your personal situation. Build your home life around Bible study and prayer; this will lead to more happiness and harmony in your home than you could ever imagine.

9. Husband must be 100 percent committed to loving his wife. Wife must be 100 percent committed to being submissive (Ephesians 5). As the husband loves his wife, she is going to be more submissive to him. As the wife submits to her husband, his love for her will surely grow. Do not marry someone who is not a Christian (2 Corinthians 6:14). Only when there is a certainty of one's trust in our Lord Jesus Christ alone for salvation can that person be considered a Christian (Acts 4:12). Only when submitting to Christ can anyone live the life-style of submission (Ephesians 5:21; 1 Corinthians 11:3).

What kind of love is a husband to bring to his wife? It is a strong, stable, mental attitude, always seeking nothing but the highest good for the one he loves. It is a love expressed in word and action which motivates the one being loved to give of herself in return.

What does it mean for a wife to be in submission to her husband? The word *submit* comes from a military term which actually means to move in an organized manner, to do an assigned job in an assigned way. Submission is the most important gift a wife can give her husband. A responsive and receptive wife willingly demonstrates that she surrenders her freedom for his love, adoration, protection, and provision.

Marriage must be a giving relationship. While the husband is giving love, giving every bit of energy, every bit of knowledge that he possesses to do that which is best for his wife and family, the wife is to respond to that love, adoration, and provision. This response will lead to an eagerness to meet her husband's needs even before he asks. It is an attitude of willing adaptation to that which God is leading her husband to do. We know submission has to be a gift from her to him because it is contrary to all natural tendencies. As it is given it releases a supernatural flow of love between the husband and the wife.

If these two attitudes of love and submission are ignored, difficulty, possibly disaster, looms ahead. If love and submission are put into action, a wonderful marriage will result, because God says very simply that this is the way He designed it.

10. The husband is to be the head of his home. "But I would have you know that the head of every man is Christ; and the head of the woman is the man; and the head of Christ is God" (1 Corinthians 11:3). "For the husband is the head of the wife, even as Christ is the head of the church. . ." (Ephesians 5:23). "One that ruleth well his own house. . ." (1 Timothy 3:4).

The husband's authority over the wife is rooted in Christ's authority over the Church. In fact, all authority we have is delegated authority, and the husband who keeps this in mind will never abuse that authority. On the other hand, the man who relinquishes his leadership position is sowing seeds which will yield trouble in due season.

The husband *is* the head of the house whether he functions in that capacity or not. Any break in the marriage relationship is the man's responsibility. Now, I did not say it was his fault. I said that God holds the man accountable for any break in the marriage, because he is the one commanded to cleave inseparably to his wife. This principle of responsibility applies in every area of the relationship, whether spiritual, emotional, or physical.

The bride-to-be should realize before the wedding how important it is to marry a man she can gladly respond to and submit to as the head of her house. I have told many young ladies, "If you cannot look up to a man, do not look at him."

11. "And the wife see that she reverence her husband" (Ephesians 5:33). What does it mean to reverence the husband? It means *to give him respect*. Fellows, it is difficult for your wife to respect you if you are not respectable. It is impossible for a woman to revere her husband if he is not worthy of reverence. The husband needs to live his life before his wife so that she can see that he is worthy of the respect God asks her to have. In the full meaning of the language of the Greek New Testament, the wife is told to respect, admire, enjoy, fear or be in awe of, defer to, revere, adore, be devoted to, esteem, praise, and deeply love her husband. This is her full-time job, and the original language of the Bible infers that she will be personally benefited as she does it.

If the wife does not trust and respect her husband, it is devastating to him and finally to the marriage. The greatest grief of love is not to be believed. But if she is able to look at her husband with eyes of reverence, he becomes a king among men!

In turn, he should give his wife the place of honor, a place of special privilege and preciousness. Many men have second-rate wives because they treat them in a second-rate manner. They never gain the real princess they would like to be married to; they just do not realize that the wife in many ways is a reflection of her husband. The wife is elevated to the position of princess by the wise and loving husband as the great principles of the God-planned marriage are put into operation.

Some of you reading this chapter have children who will be entering marriage in a few years. And you want to do all you can to prepare them for a good marriage. Let me make these suggestions:

The most important thing a father can do for his children is to love their mother. The home should be the most attractive place in the world to the children, and the mother should be the greatest attraction.

Without a warm atmosphere in your home and marriage—an atmosphere of love, of generosity, of forgiveness—your children will not know how to love. The only person who knows how to love is the person who has been loved, who has seen love, who has experienced love. The Christian home is a laboratory in which the love of God is demonstrated.

If you do not have this kind of love in your home, your children are likely to grow up with a feeling of inferiority, emptiness, and lack of worth. But it is not too late for you to develop this. It is never too late for two people who want a transformed marriage. Remember that the only course on marriage most children will ever take is the one at home! As fathers and mothers in a Christian home, we can provide the best in marriage preparation for our children by having a genuine love for one another and by learning all we can about how to express that love, so our children will have a visible ongoing demonstration of real love.

I have had the opportunity as a family doctor to see results in the marriages of the couples who received this kind of premarriage counseling based upon the absolutes of the Word of God. Over a period of years I have watched the couples who have applied these principles develop stable, loving, satisfying relationships. *These basic instructions from the Bible, if followed, will ensure happy marriages.*

Applying heavenly principles to a marriage can produce a heaven on earth. This is my desire for every young couple and for every home.

3

What If I'm Not in Love?
How Do I Fall in Love?

Sex within the marriage of a man and woman who *love* one another can be like a precious stone shining and sparkling in the perfect setting.

But what if you're married and feel that you no longer love your partner? Is it possible to change your feelings? Is there any hope of finding sexual fulfillment together?

This question has been asked of me many times. My answer is a simple *yes*. Yes, you can change your feelings. Yes, there is still hope of finding sexual fulfillment with your mate. This chapter tells you how. But we have to begin by defining what love itself is.

This becomes a difficult task when we find that the Oxford English Dictionary takes five pages to define *love* without much success even after all that. Ask a hundred people for a definition of love, and the chances are good that you will get at least ninety different answers.

Obviously the world has no clear-cut definition of love. Meanings of the word vary according to individual experiences and viewpoints. Love can be passion, affection, romantic feelings, friendship, fondness, infatuation, or innumerable combinations of those qualities. But almost always, *love* as the world uses it includes an expectation of getting something in return.

The Bible reveals another kind of love which the world does not understand, and it is this kind of love which provides the perfect setting for the "one flesh" experience of sex in marriage. The New Testament calls it *agape* love and so fully pictures it in word and action that as

31

Christians we can begin to comprehend it, though we cannot plumb its depths.

Agape love is unconditional and irrevocable. God chose to love us first, before we gave Him our love in return, or even knew who He was. Agape love gives without measuring the cost or seeking personal advantage. "For God so loved the world that he gave His only begotten Son, that whosoever believeth in him should not perish, but have everlasting life" (John 3:16). Agape love is not natural; it is supernatural! It is a love poured out upon us in a beautiful abundance, seeking nothing but our highest good. It does not depend upon our actions. While God deeply desires our response, our reaction to Him has no bearing on *whether* He will love us. That is already decided. He does love us; He has made the irrevocable choice to love us; and He has proved it by giving His best to us—His Son.

Agape love has something both glorious and practical to say to the married couple, for it is this amazing way of loving, *God's way*, which can become *our* way of loving by God's power. The principles of agape love operating in the marriage relationship can answer every need, solve every problem, and show us the way to regions of joy unending.

The New Testament writings show us that agape love in the marriage must involve total commitment, just as God is totally committed to us. God's command is for Adam to "cleave" to Eve. "Therefore shall a man leave his father and his mother and shall cleave unto his wife. And they shall be one flesh" (Genesis 2:24). This means that even before God expects man to love his mate He expects him to be totally committed to her. Deep in our minds and hearts as man and wife, there needs to be an irrevocable commitment to the marriage.

With today's come-and-go marriages, total commitment would seem to be out of date. But perhaps we have allowed the world to set our expectations for us, making divorce the norm instead of the exception. There are still plenty of people who get married intending their relationship to be permanent; but with a 50 percent divorce rate in parts of our nation, some of those people have failed somewhere. Perhaps part of the problem is a lack of commitment to commitment!

"To cherish in sickness and in health" should remind a couple that in marriage storms may blow up and have to be ridden out. If we think in terms of a foreseeable time when things will be tough enough to quit, quitting becomes an alternative. Often it is all too short a step from possibility to probability. Jesus' statement: "What, therefore, God hath joined together, let not man put asunder" (Mark 10:9) needs to become such a part of our thinking that full commitment to marriage, no matter what, will be our only option. In other words, when we go into marriage it should be with the conviction that *there is no way out*. Then both partners will be committed to making the marriage a success.

But far too many couples come to the painful point of admitting, "We don't love each other anymore." When they say it they assume, of course, that the marriage must be over. This attitude indicates that the couple had a misplaced confidence in the world's vague idea of love and suggests that God's way of loving never existed there in the first place.

The fact is, the Bible gives no indication that the feeling the world calls love is to be the foundation for marriage. A marriage built entirely upon this will be characterized by fluctuating feelings as the circumstances change. Result: shaky emotions, shaky marriage!

Emotions do not and never will sustain a marriage. There are those cold grey mornings of life when one awakens emotionally weary; obviously, emotions cannot be depended upon for stability in marriage. And we do not have to be helpless slaves to love or any other emotion that we slip into or fall out of. But as commitment binds husband and wife together through shared happiness and trouble, all the wonderful, pleasurable emotions they could wish for will spring forth from agape love in action. Commitment is the bond; the feeling of love is the result. The *feeling* comes because of the *fact* of commitment through every changing circumstance.

Marriage does not necessarily make people happy. But people can make their marriage a happy one by giving to one another, working together, serving together, and growing together. Or they can allow the marriage to disintegrate by not doing these things.

We have all experienced times when we actively pursued happiness for ourselves. We found that it seemed to run away from us like a startled deer in the woods as soon as we could see it almost within grasp. Most of us know by now that happiness can never be caught when we chase it. Instead, it comes to us freely, surprisingly, when we are concentrating on something else and least expect it. If we grab for emotional happiness without committing and giving first, our selfishness will reap only misery and coldness. But an honest desire for the happiness of our partner will bring a surprising degree of happiness into our own lives—a fringe benefit based on the principles of God's Word: "Give and it shall be given unto you, good measure, pressed down and shaken together, and running over" (Luke 6:38).

Love, in essence, is that deliberate act of giving one's self to another so that the other person constantly receives enjoyment. Love gives, and love's richest reward comes when the object of love responds to the gift of one's self. If a man and wife so give themselves for each other, each will have a sense of completeness and contentment. Not only that! The conditions have then become right for building a love relationship which will bring to the marriage all the richly delightful feelings of being in love. Agape love is always the fertile soil for God-planned pleasure in the physical marriage relationship.

God so designed us that we cannot be truly satisfied with mere physical and physiological relief in sex. The world which often tries to view love and sex in marriage as two separate entities has missed the point. In God's perfect design it is in a marriage characterized by agape love that all the emotions of loving increase and multiply. We find our greatest satisfaction in becoming one with our beloved, in both possessing and serving the beloved. Yet love is not a fixed thing, although the context of commitment never changes. From day to day, even from hour to hour, within the framework of commitment, our emotions of loving may change. At one time physical desire may be paramount. At other times, desire for affection and close companionship may be the only element present. Sex desire as a conscious need will arise sometimes only after intimate time has been spent together. But if we have entered into God's way of loving, we will know a blessed security together in the midst of life with all its perplexing changes and unexpected demands upon us. Love, God's kind of love, is the answer!

Love Renewal in the Marriage

The couples who assume their marriage is over because they no longer love one another need to know that no matter what has occurred in the past, agape love which God makes available to the believer can renew and transform their marriage in every area, touching the smallest practical details of daily life and improving the physical relationship to an amazing degree.

Renewal of love takes place in three areas: choice of the will, action, and feeling. Note that feeling comes last, because the *feeling* of love is not the crucial ingredient of the marriage, but the *fact* of love based on an unchanging commitment to the other person.

Renewal of love begins in your mind, where your will exercises the choice and makes the decision to love no matter what—and never to stop loving. Here the wounds you and your partner have suffered must be dealt with first. Where the feelings of love have departed, all the unhappy emotions—anger, guilt, hurt, resentment or bitterness—are sure to be lurking in the shadows. Find them and send them packing! They deserve nothing but dismissal, for they will give you nothing but grief. You and your partner need to realize that there must be open communication, which is healing in nature when it springs from total forgiveness. Let it begin with you. Start by admitting that your loss of love is a result of wanting to receive rather than wanting to give. Recognize that you can be the instrument through whom God Himself will communicate His love to your partner. Pray and commit yourself to this. Thank God in advance for the supernatural agape love which will flow through you as He promised.

This love which must be learned, which starts in the mind, which is subject to the will, not the emotions, always results in *action*. Love becomes something we *do*, before it is something we *feel*. Thus we choose to demonstrate and initiate love.

How we show our love is vitally important. God has given certain specific guidelines on the part the husband and wife each are to have in the marriage relationship. The husband, according to Scripture, is the leader and the lover, while the wife is the helper and the responder. This intertwining nature of love and response or submission which is so crucial may become obscured in the day of strident voices for the ''liberation'' of women. God has designed the relationship of husband and wife with an understanding of their unique strengths and differences so that the husband delights in loving a wife who is submissive and responsive; a wife gladly submits to a husband who loves in God's way. But neither can *demand* the appropriate response from the other. It must be a gift. The wonderful thing is, it can start with either partner. The wife wants to obey a truly loving, caring, protective husband. Her resulting submission makes him love her all the more, and he will want to reciprocate with whatever will make her happy. Her quick response causes him to love her more, and the cycle goes on and on—gloriously.

The husband must be 100 percent committed to loving his wife. "Husbands, love your wives, even as Christ also loved the Church, and gave Himself for it" (Ephesians 5:25). The wife must be 100 percent committed to being submissive to her husband. "Therefore, as the Church is subject to Christ, so let the wives be to their own husbands in everything" (Ephesians 5:24).

Some people talk of marriage as ideally a 50/50 proposition. The problem with this idea is that each partner is always waiting for the other to do something first. With a 100/100 partnership, either partner acting with a 100 percent giving attitude will contribute to the total marriage so that there will be a reciprocating love from the other partner.

The submissive role of the wife implies that whether the husband acts like it or not, he is responsible for the important decisions in the home. "For the husband is the head of the wife, even as Christ is the head of the Church. . ." (Ephesians 5:23). This is not to demote or put down the wife. Rather, it takes an unnecessary load from her. If the wife assumes the responsibilities the husband has neglected, she takes on pressures she was never created to cope with. The husband is allowed to escape his responsibilities, and the family structure deteriorates. This has occurred in many American homes today.

Love is the preeminent characteristic of the emotionally mature person, because as 1 Corinthians 13 says, "Love seeketh not its own." Therefore the wise husband who truly loves his wife will maturely shoulder his responsibilities. The wise wife who truly loves her husband will not demand her rights when he asks something of her. If she maturely loves her husband she will not need to try to defend her self-image. She will seek to please. In fact, she will try to please her husband creatively, and do his will even before he asks—just as the husband will look for creative ways to express his love to her even before she shows any obvious need for reassurance.

If you choose to love according to God's way of loving, you will find yourself watching for needs you can meet in your mate. God will show you specific needs, actual needs which you can rejoice in meeting. And what you sow you will reap. (*See* Galatians 6:7–10.) What you give will be returned to you. These divine principles will prove themselves again and again in the realm of your marriage.

Although this can begin with either partner, I want to address the husbands with some specific applications of these principles.

Husband, if you want to learn *how* to love your wife all over again, start by giving to her, knowing that the agape love of God is energizing you. As you give yourself (your time, your attention, your caring), your feelings of love for her will grow. You have been instructed in Ephesians 5 to give yourself sacrificially to your wife in the same way that Christ gave Himself to the Church. In other words, He loved enough to die for the Church. How often a husband who says he would give his life to save the life of his wife in a moment of danger does not have time to give himself daily to her emotional, physical, and spiritual needs! You must give—give first, give generously, and continue to give—if you hope to experience the expanding joys of love. If you are not giving, you are merely taking. There is no natural momentum to keep a marriage going, apart from the powerful force of giving to one another. Keep in mind that the opposite of love is not hate but *indifference*.

Now, husband, how do you initiate love? Coming home from work you can either be grumpy from the day's pressures, or you can come into the house cheerfully and with an attitude of concern and respect for what your wife has experienced during the day. A wise friend says he has picked a certain stoplight between his office and home where he dumps his office problems and tensions and refuses to pick them up again until the next day. To bring problems home with you and try to escape behind a newspaper or the television set does not demonstrate love for your wife.

Conveying the attitude of concern for her builds the right atmosphere for satisfaction in sex. After all, most men can begin sexual intercourse after a bad day, a family argument, with worries galore, or with supper burning on the stove! But your wife will respond much more readily when motivated by respect and consideration on the part of her husband. She needs an introductory period of sensitive consideration, and without that she cannot fully respond in a satisfying physical relationship. Building an atmosphere of caring and romance is a sign of true love on the part of the husband.

A woman's emotional makeup requires verbal expression from her husband to assure her of continuing love and security. You should be wise enough to know this about your wife and loving enough to do it. You can build up her self-esteem just through your words to her. Words have power! There are so many ways a man can show his love and regard for his wife. Say it with a card or candy or flowers. But by all means say it with words. There is the tired joke about the husband who said, "In ten years of married life the reason I never told my wife I loved her is because I told her in our marriage vows, and I haven't taken it back yet.'' This is not only a bad joke; it is unfortunately a living reality to all too many couples.

Another aspect of loving your partner involves thanking God for every good quality in her. People often complain about the undesirable qualities in their mates, while overlooking those qualities which originally attracted them to one another. Agape love in marriage expresses by word and action, thought and prayer, the deepest appreciation for our partner, with the intense awareness of his or her needs and longings, past, present, and future.

Love in action on the part of both marriage partners involves physical touching. In fact, because the greatest desire of love is to find an answering love, there is nothing that can so quickly build or rebuild the intense feeling of love in marriage than repeatedly reaching out to a responding partner and having that one lovingly reach back to you with tender touching—both of you gently drawing closer and closer, cuddling and snuggling and fondling.

This is vividly illustrated by our teenagers who spend too much time in close physical contact, causing their relationship to become a helpless enslavement to an overwhelming emotion, unable to see any defects, attributing all that is desirable and admirable to one another, and generating a blind compulsion to possess one another.

Oh, that more Christian married couples could learn a lesson from this occurrence and use loving physical communication to attain greater oneness within their own marriages by giving to each other more and more intimate physical attention. The sexual relationship is perhaps the most logical place for both husband and wife to begin giving to each other.

As you read this book and gain new understanding and knowledge of the sexual relationship, you will find that obstacles in the physical area are being removed, and your love which was previously hindered is now being freed. The more freely you express your affection in physical terms of touching and pleasuring the other, the more love you will ''feel'' for your marriage partner. The physical expressions of affection will allow the love emotion which was previously blocked to be liberated. The feeling of love which had been hopelessly buried under defenses and weapons can emerge from its protective shell to bless the marriage in a most wonderful way.

The renewal of love starts with a choice of the will, a commitment to love, followed by actions which demonstrate loving concern, and the feeling of love naturally follows. And so feeling is the third stage in the process. Remember that it is easier to change actions than it is to change feelings. As your actions become markedly different, you will discover that the desired feelings are following closely behind.

Renewal of love in marriage can be the springboard to experiencing the joys of the "one flesh" relationship as God planned it to be in the beginning.

4

Understanding the Basics

Any helpful discussion of the physical relationship between husband and wife needs to begin with the basic facts of human anatomy. You must understand these in order to apply the sex techniques described in following chapters. Perhaps you are familiar with many of these facts already, or at least have some awareness of them from health and hygiene courses, but please go over the material carefully. Even one error or bit of misinformation concerning reproductive and sexual functions could lead to a less than satisfactory relationship in your marriage. These "basics" include an explanation of medical problems which directly affect sexual activity. Newlyweds will be particularly interested in the instructions for the wedding night.

We are presenting this specialized knowledge in words and illustrations which can be easily understood. Parents, you will find this section helpful in preparing for the time when your children are old enough to begin seeking information. The truth given here is expressed in language as specific, but as simple and discreet, as the complex nature of this subject will permit.

To begin at the beginning, we must start with names, the proper vocabulary for discussion of sexual functions.

The mystery connected with the giving of names traces back to Adam's job of naming the animals in the Garden (Genesis 2:20). That naming was somehow the first step toward having "dominion" over the earth. You will find that knowing the correct names of sexual organs and functions is

41

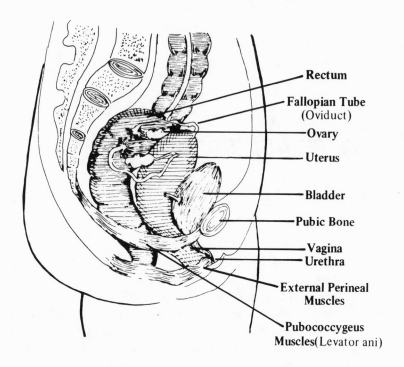

Rectum

Fallopian Tube
(Oviduct)

Ovary

Uterus

Bladder

Pubic Bone

Vagina
Urethra

External Perineal
Muscles

Pubococcygeus
Muscles(Levator ani)

Figure I

Side view of female reproductive system

Especially note the location of P.C. muscles which provide an
important part of the support for the reproductive organs. Controlled
contraction of these muscles gives added sexual pleasure for both
husband and wife.

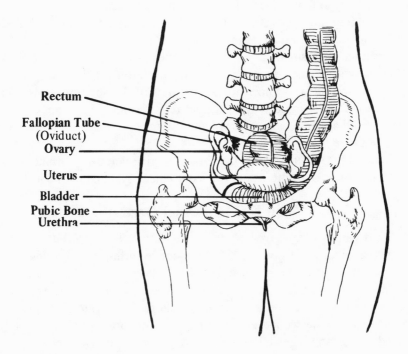

Rectum

Fallopian Tube
(Oviduct)
Ovary

Uterus

Bladder
Pubic Bone
Urethra

Figure II

Front view of female reproductive system

This shows the relationship between the various organs of reproduction.
Notice here and in Figure I that the urethra lies between the vagina and
the pubic bone. Thus it can be easily bruised during coitus.

the first step to real understanding of the sex relationship. Many people have been handicapped by the wrong vocabulary, by words that are embarrassing to think of, let alone use. The right names will give you and your children a proper appreciation of the sanctity and dignity of God's provision for pleasure in marriage.

When we meet someone for the first time, we generally want to know: What is your name? then, Where are you from? What do you do? Likewise, we need to know not only names of the sex organs, but also their locations, specific functions, and relationships to one another. All this, as well as some medical problems that may arise in certain organs, is included here.

Remember as you read that our goal is to give you the information that will lead you into a more wonderful experience of all that marriage offers.

The Female Sexual Organs

The organs that can give genesis to life are called the *genitalia*, a Latin word that means "to give birth." The female birth-giving organs are in two groups. One group is outside the body and easily visible; it is called the external genitalia. The *vulva* (Latin for *covering*) is the collective name for the entire group of female external genital organs. This group is the gateway to the second group of reproductive organs inside the body, called the internal genitalia. These are made up of two ovaries, two oviducts (tubes), the uterus, and the vagina. (*See* Figures I and II, pages 42, 43.)

The reproductive organs are formed several months before one's own birth but remain inactive until puberty (usually age twelve to fifteen), when they receive the signal to come to sexual maturity. This important signal is given by the pituitary, a small gland situated at the base of the brain.

Pituitary Gland (pĭ tū ′ ĭ tā ry).   The pituitary gland lies in a bony saddle of the skull, under the brain and near the middle of the head. It is no larger than a small lima bean, yet it is a major control gland that sends chemical "signals" through the bloodstream to other parts of the body. These signals are in the form of chemical substances called hormones. Through a complex relay system, these pituitary hormones control many functions, including growth of bone and body.

Recent medical research indicates that the pituitary gland responds to signals from a part of the brain called the hypothalamus. This means that the amount of some of our hormones can be indirectly, but partially, governed by what we think or by our attitudes.

At puberty, a girl's pituitary actively secretes two main female hormones that arouse the reproductive organs to maturity. The internal organs, which lie inside the protective pelvic bones, begin their response just before the external organs of sex give evidence of beginning maturity.

Ovaries (ō ' vå rēs). The word *ovary* comes from the Latin word *ova*, which means eggs. The ovaries are the main target organs for the pituitary hormones. At puberty the pituitary secretions carried by the bloodstream signal the ovaries to begin to develop eggs. Soon the ovaries will be in full production to continue for thirty or more years.

There are two ovaries, each suspended near the internal center of the lower body about four to five inches below the waist, halfway between the back of the pelvis and the groin. Each ovary is about the size of a robin's egg. At the time of puberty, the surface of the ovary is smooth. Shimmering through the surface there are many tiny glistening droplets called follicles. Each of these ovarian follicles holds an immature egg, or ovum, that is the female cell of reproduction. The eggs in the droplets are so small they would be only barely visible. They are smaller than the dot on an *i*, and it would take at least two million of them to fill a sewing thimble.

The ovaries have another equally vital function: to produce at least two important hormones of their own. These work together with the pituitary hormones to bring the rest of the reproductive system to maturity and then to keep it in working order.

When a baby girl is born there are about 300,000 to 400,000 follicles in the ovaries, although only about 300 to 400 eggs will ever actually reach maturity and be released from the ovary. If two ova, or eggs, are released at one time and both ova are fertilized, a twin pregnancy may result. These babies would not be identical twins, but would be fraternal twins—merely brothers or sisters born at nearly the same time. Identical twins come from the division of a single fertilized egg, and this always produces identical babies of the same sex.

Oviducts (ō ' vĭ dŭkts). The word *oviducts* means "egg ducts." These are also commonly called the fallopian tubes. There are two oviducts, or tubes—one for each ovary. Primarily made of muscle, each of these tubes is about four inches long, and about the same diameter as a small telephone cord.

These muscular oviducts are essential to the transport of the tiny immobile eggs from the ovaries. At the same time, the oviducts provide the meeting ground for the female egg and male sperm which are coming to each other from opposite directions.

An egg coming from the ovary must first of all be caught by the oviduct. Neither oviduct is directly attached to its ovary. Instead, each oviduct has a trumpet-shaped widened opening near the ovary. This opening is rimmed with fingerlike fringes *(fimbria)* that conduct a sweeping motion which carries all before it into the oviduct. After the egg is taken into the opening of the oviduct by the sweeping fringe, waves of muscular contractions continue to aid its transport downstream toward the womb.

The trumpet-shaped opening of the oviduct leads to a passage that is no wider than this hyphen: (-). This internal passage, about the size of the point of a pencil, is lined with minute clumps of brushlike hairs called *cilia*. The size of the cilia, in proportion to the egg, is like that of eyelashes in comparison to an orange. The cilia are the sweepers that help to keep the egg gently flowing toward the womb.

An infection, particularly a venereal infection, may block these fallopian tubes by scarring them on the inside. This may cause a woman to be unable to have children. Sometimes these obstructions can be removed by careful surgery. Tubal obstructions are seen by injecting a liquid which shows clearly on X-rays as it flows through the *os*, or mouth, of the cervix, into the uterus and through the tubes. This is called a salpingogram and can be done in a doctor's office or in any hospital X-ray department on an outpatient basis. This procedure may cause some slight pain and discomfort, but nothing that is unbearable. It requires no anesthesia.

In performing sterilization for birth control, the surgeon usually double-ties each tube with silk thread and then removes a section of each of these oviducts or tubes. This requires the opening of the abdomen and is thus a major operation requiring several days' stay in the hospital. However, there is another method which does not require the wife to be hospitalized. Some physicians are able to do laparoscopic surgery in which a Laparoscope, a small lighted tube instrument, is passed through an incision in the area just below the navel. Through another small incision in the lower abdomen another instrument is inserted with which the surgeon is able to grasp and manipulate each oviduct. While he watches through the Laparoscope, a loop of the oviduct is grasped and an electrocautery tip is used to burn and do away with about one or two inches of the mid portion of each oviduct. There are some other techniques used to close these oviducts, and one of the simplest ones is to insert through the small lower abdominal incision an instrument with which the oviduct can be manipulated, grasped, and pulled up into a loop, a small circular elastic ring (similar to a small rubber band) being then slipped over this elevated loop, thus very tightly squeezing the oviduct closed in two places. At present the elastic-ring method probably offers the best possibility for success of later surgery to reconstruct the tubes, if the woman decides at a future time that she wants to have another baby. I would not, however, want to convey the idea that any operative sterilization method is reversible. An operation for sterilization should be considered as permanent sterilization. Reconstruction surgery would be a very tedious and delicate major operation and would certainly cause some discomfort.

By describing these methods, I am merely explaining for you how and why certain techniques of birth control work. Whether or not you practice family planning is your decision and yours alone. However, every married couple is entitled to have information about each method of birth control when making this decision.

Uterus (ū ′ tĕr ŭs). The Latin word *uterus* means womb or belly. The uterus, usually the size and shape of a small pear, is firm and muscular. It is about four inches long. When the woman is standing, it is suspended in a nearly horizontal position in the body so that the small end of the pear points toward the tip of the spine, while the bulbous upper end points forward.

During pregnancy, the uterus can expand greatly to accommodate, as we know, up to six babies. This is possible because the uterus has many elastic fibers meshed in with the powerful muscle fibers. These muscles later play an important part in labor by contracting forcefully to deliver the baby.

The outside of the uterus is flesh pink in color. Inside there is a red

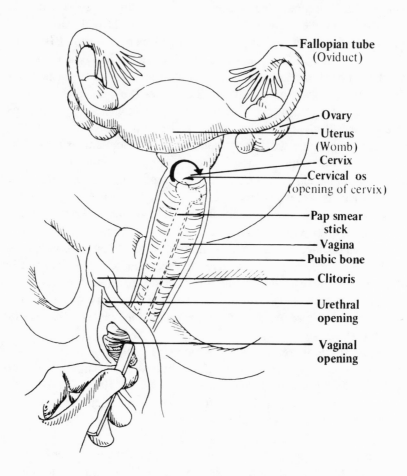

Figure III

Obtaining a Pap smear from the cervix

This simple and painless procedure helps to save many lives annually, as it detects cervical cancer before it can be seen with the eye.

velvety lining called endometrium, from the Greek "within the womb."

Within the uterus is a narrow triangular cavity surrounded by thick muscular walls. An intrauterine device, commonly called an IUD, can be placed in this cavity as a means of preventing pregnancy.

The two incoming oviduct canals enter at the top of the uterine cavity. The lower part of the uterine cavity that forms the narrowest base is called the cervical canal.

Cervix (sûr ' vĭks).   The word *cervix* means neck in Latin, referring to the neck of the uterus. Surrounding the cervical canal, the cervix forms the narrow lower end of the uterus. It can be easily examined by the physician since about half the cervix projects into the vagina.

Like the rest of the uterus, the cervix is firm and muscular. Medical students are sometimes taught that before the first pregnancy the cervix feels like the tip of the nose, and after childbirth it feels like the point of the chin.

The *cervical os* is the opening of the cervix into the vagina. This passageway is as narrow as the lead in a pencil and is framed by strong muscles. Only under strong pressure, as in childbirth, does the fibroelastic tissue of the cervix dilate to increase the size of the opening. The normally tight passage helps to keep the interior of the uterus virtually germfree, especially since a constant slight current of cleansing moisture flows outward.

This moisture, along with a light scraping of cervical cells, is examined for cancer cells in the Papanicolaou, or Pap, smear. It is recommended that women have a Pap smear about once each year, as the cervix is the site of most of the cancer of the female organs. It takes two to six days to get a final report on the Pap smear. When cervical cancer is found early, more than 90 percent is curable with correct treatment. (*See* Figure III, page 48.)

Vagina (và jī ' nà).   The word *vagina* means sheath in Latin. The vagina is a very elastic, sheathlike canal that serves as a passage to and from the sheltered genital organs inside the body. At its upper end, the vagina forms a curving vault that encloses the tip of the cervix. The inner walls of the vagina consist of folds of tissue which tend to lie in contact. The vagina, normally three to five inches long, can expand easily to receive the penis. Its greatest expansion, of course, occurs during childbirth. The folds contain many tiny glands which continuously pro-

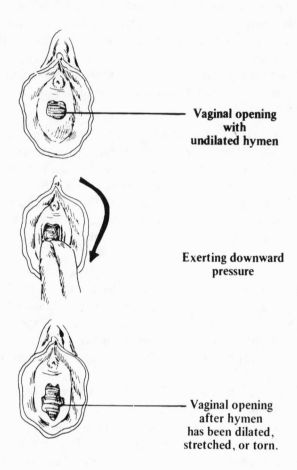

Figure IV

Stretching the hymen

This procedure can be done by the physician or by the bridegroom to avoid discomfort during the first intercourse. Observe that finger pressure should be downward and toward the back.

duce a cleansing film of moisture so that the vagina is self-cleansing. For this reason douches are seldom necessary.

The external perineal muscles encircle the vaginal opening where a concentration of sensory nerves play a significant role in sexual arousal when stimulated by touch.

Lubrication of the vagina usually occurs seconds after sexual arousal begins. This appears as beads of lubricant covering the walls of the vagina much as moisture on a cold glass. Knowing the location of this natural lubrication aids intercourse when the husband learns to reach up into the vagina and gently bring some of this lubricant to the mouth of the vagina before inserting the penis. If there is not sufficient natural lubrication, a couple may use an artificial lubricant such as Johnson & Johnson's K-Y Jelly, which is obtainable at any drugstore. Just a tiny amount need be applied to the head of the penis or to the outside of the vagina.

The vagina is not passive but is a very active organ which when sexually stimulated increases in length and widens to twice its diameter. At the beginning of arousal the upper vagina expands, and the uterus lifts up toward the abdomen. When thrusting begins, the vagina constricts to conform to the penis. After orgasm the uterus moves downward, so that the cervix rests in a pool of semen deposited in the upper vagina.

Hymen (hī ' měn).   The name of the mythical god of marriage, *hymen*, has been given to the membrane at the back of the opening of the vagina. This membrane may be relatively tough, or it may even be absent from birth. Its absence is not necessarily an indication of loss of virginity.

At the time of their first experience of intercourse, two out of every ten brides have no pain at all, but five out of every ten brides have some pain, and three out of ten have rather severe pain. This is because the opening in the hymen of the virgin is about one inch in diameter, but about one and a half inch is needed for comfortable intercourse.

About six weeks before marriage, every woman should have a complete physical examination. A thoughtful, interested physician can help remove much of her fear of physical pain due to intercourse. If a pelvic examination before marriage reveals a thick or tight hymen, the prospective bride may wish to have this tissue stretched so there will be less difficulty and discomfort during the first intercourse. The physician can do this, or she may wish to use her own fingers to stretch the membrane herself, or she may ask for specific instructions for her future husband to do this after marriage. (*See* Figure IV, page 50.)

On the wedding night, if the bride chooses to have her husband dilate her hymen, a lubricating jelly must be applied to the penis and around the vaginal outlet. An intercourse position should be chosen so that the penis is directed downward and toward the back of the vaginal opening. The bride should be the one to do the thrusting, as she will be better able to control the amount of pressure. It may take several tries to penetrate the hymen. If unsuccessful after a few trials, the couple should simply caress each other's genital areas until sexually satisfied. The area should not be painfully bruised by repeated attempts at penetration.

If at the time of the pelvic examination before marriage the physician has advised that the vaginal outlet seems to be too tight because of a thick or resistant hymen, the bride may wish to ask for a prescription for a local-anesthetic ointment, or she may purchase Nupercainal ointment from any druggist without a prescription. The Nupercainal ointment should be gently applied around the vaginal opening, especially toward the back, for a period of five minutes before attempting to stretch the hymen.

To dilate the vaginal opening the husband must use generous amounts of artificial lubricant on his fingers, making sure his nails are filed short and smooth. One finger should be gently inserted into the vagina, then two fingers. The husband should push with a gradual, firm, downward pressure toward the anus until there is definite pain and both fingers can be inserted all the way to the base of the fingers. If this stretching is too painful, it is better to wait until the next day before attempting inter-course. Most pain occurs from too quick an entry by the penis, before the muscles around the vagina have had time to relax.

If the husband is unsuccessful after several attempts, the couple should again see their family physician. He may need to make small incisions in the hymen at the back and on each side. This procedure is done using a local anesthetic. The incisions will heal within a week (as will any other small tear in the hymen).

At the time of first intercourse, the husband should not strive to bring his wife to orgasm with his penis in the vagina. She will have some soreness, and there is no reason to make this worse. After the penis is inserted, the husband should have his orgasm quickly, withdraw the penis, and stimulate his wife gently with his fingers to bring her to orgasm.

Bleeding often occurs when the hymen is stretched or torn, but usually no more than one or two teaspoons of blood. Do not be afraid—simply look for the exact spot that is bleeding and hold a Kleenex on the spot with a firm pressure. All bleeding can be stopped in this way. The tissue may be left in place about twelve hours and then soaked loose in warm water to avoid new bleeding. Intercourse can begin again the next day. If bleeding occurs again, repeat the local pressure.

The objectives of your first few weeks of sexual encounters should be maximum feminine comfort and maximum masculine control. Don't expect much harmony in sexual intercourse for at least a few weeks.

Urethra (ū rē ′ thrȧ). The *urethra* is the small tube through which the urine drains from the bladder. The urethral opening is about one-half inch above the vaginal opening and entirely separate from the vagina. It protrudes slightly and contains a tiny slit.

The urethra lies just beneath the pubic bone and is easily bruised, especially in the first few days after marriage, unless sufficient lubrication is provided for the penis in the vagina. This bruising results in what commonly is called "newlywed cystitis" or "honeymoon cystitis." This is characterized by pain in the bladder area, blood in the urine, and by severe burning while urinating. Bruising of the urethra has allowed bacteria to grow there. The infection may ascend to produce a severe bladder infection. This can be cleared up quickly with medication prescribed by a physician and by drinking more fluids. Since the infection is caused by bacteria from the vagina being pushed into the urethra during intercourse, a wife who has *repeated* attacks of cystitis may be able to help avoid them by urinating within a few minutes after each intercourse. Her urine can thus rinse away the bacteria before they can produce infection. In prevention of frequent cystitis, it may also be helpful before each sexual union to remove bacteria by thoroughly washing the vulva with a washcloth, using soap and water.

Clitoris (klī ′ tō rĭs; klĭt ō rĭs).   This word is Latin for "that which is closed in." Closed in by the peak of the labia, the shaft of the clitoris is from one-half to one inch long and is located about one inch above the entrance to the vagina. Its outer end is a small, rounded body about the size of a pea and is called the glans. A fold of skin called the prepuce (prē ′ pyōōs) partly covers the glans. (*See* Figure V, page 54.)

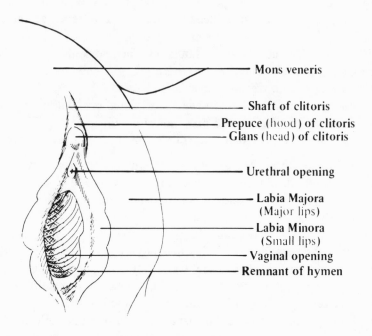

Mons veneris

Shaft of clitoris
Prepuce (hood) of clitoris
Glans (head) of clitoris

Urethral opening

Labia Majora
(Major lips)
Labia Minora
(Small lips)
Vaginal opening
Remnant of hymen

Figure V

Vulva or external female organs (external genitalia)

The area between the urethral opening and the upper shaft of the clitoris is the most sexually sensitive region of a woman's body. During arousal the labia minora swell and the size of the vaginal opening decreases.

The clitoris has been called the trigger of female desire. It is the most keenly sensitive point a woman has for sexual arousal and has, as far as we know, no other function. Sufficient physical stimulation of the clitoris alone will produce orgasm in nearly all women. For this reason, many have thought that contact between the penis and clitoris is the only important factor in achieving orgasm. Many operations have been performed to provide greater exposure of the clitoris. Yet, such surgery seldom helps attain orgasm. With our present knowledge, this surgery should not be considered until the information in this book has been digested and applied in the sex relationship. If sexual stimulation causes pain in the clitoris, there may be some rock-hard particles of dried secretion (smegma) beneath some adhesions of the prepuce. These particles can be easily removed and the adhesions released using a small metal probe. This is a simple procedure which is done in the doctor's office.

The clitoris usually enlarges somewhat when caressed, but there is no need for anxiety if it does not. In a study of hundreds of women able to reach orgasm, more than half showed no visible enlargement of the clitoris. Enlargement was only barely noticeable by either sight or touch in others. Most of the enlargement is in diameter, not in length. The size of the clitoris, or its enlargement, has nothing to do with sexual satisfaction or sexual capacity. Two important points are:

1. The clitoris *must* be stimulated either directly or indirectly for the wife to achieve orgasm.
2. There is no difference in *physical* sensation of orgasm whether by clitoral stimulation or from sexual intercourse.

When the clitoris is first stimulated in foreplay, very light, gentle, slow caressing usually gives the most satisfaction. In a few seconds the glans often becomes overly sensitive or even irritated, and stroking further back on the shaft or at the side of the shaft will probably give a more pleasurable sensation. Some wives even prefer to be stimulated in an entirely different area, such as the breasts, or the inner thighs, before returning to the areas near the clitoris.

Labia Minora (lā ′ bǐ ä   mǐ nōr ′ ä). The *labia minora* is Latin for "small lips." They are two parallel folds of smooth, hairless, soft tissue that connect to the hood over the clitoris and end just below the entrance to the vagina. During sexual arousal these lips expand two or three times their normal thickness. Gentle stroking of these small lips gives a more pleasant sensation than stroking the clitoris. Since these lips are connected directly above the clitoris, when the penis moves in the vagina there is friction, tugging and pulling, which carries sensation to the clitoris. Therefore, direct stimulation of the clitoris is not always desired or necessary to increase sexual enjoyment.

A man will be at least 85 percent wrong if he thinks he knows exactly what his wife likes in sexual stimulation. Thus, every husband should discard the thought that he is an expert. The really wise husband will know he does not know and will look to his wife for specific direction for her stimulation. By communicating verbally or by subtle signals, the wife should indicate what stimulation gives her the most pleasure. This communication should be done lovingly as needed at any given point in foreplay or in achieving orgasm.

Labia Majora (lā ′ bǐ ä   må jōr ′ ä). *Labia majora* is Latin for "major lips." They lie outside and parallel to the labia minora. They are normally over the vaginal opening and provide protection against entrance of the penis or other objects into the unstimulated vagina. With sexual arousal, the major lips lie back and flatten.

Mons Veneris (mŏnz   věn ′ ěr ĭs). *Mons veneris* is Latin for "Mount of Venus." It is a small cushion of fat which serves as a shock absorber over the pubic symphysis (the bony prominence above the labia majora).

The Menstrual Cycle

The menstrual (měn ′ stroo ăl) cycle prepares, renews, and refreshes the reproductive system for thirty to forty years of a woman's life. Continuous daily activity, mostly unseen and unfelt, occurs in these organs as a result of the stimulation of the female hormones. Until recently this activity was not well understood. Today it is, and this has made possible many advances in the control of conception and in the treatment of menstrual irregularities and infertility.

Only one step of the whole cycle has always made itself plainly known: menstruation. Named for the Latin word *mensis*, meaning month, it is an approximately monthly shedding of the lining of the uterus. Menstruation makes way for a new lining and is the only instance in nature where a loss of blood does not signify injury but is, instead, a sign of good health. We might mention here that the word *menopause* has the obvious meaning of a pause in menstruation.

How Menstruation Begins (měn ' strōō ā ' shŭn). The first day of the menstrual flow is counted as "Day 1" of the menstrual cycle. On the day that the menstrual flow starts, the inner lining of the uterine cavity has grown to be nearly twice as deep as it was after the last menstruation.

The menstrual flow is caused by the shedding of the thickened lining. The shedding takes place because the supply of certain hormones is discontinued. These hormones are called estrogen and progesterone.

The fully developed lining is composed of thousands of microscopically small blood vessels, with millions of cells of a soft spongy tissue packed around them. The blood vessels act as a support and at the same time carry nourishment to the tissues. These soft tissues, rich in blood supply, have stood in readiness for the possible arrival of a fertilized egg. Had there been a fertilized egg, the supply of the one hormone, progesterone (meaning "for gestation or pregnancy"), would have continued to maintain the lining and prevent menstruation.

When the supply of hormones stops, growth of the lining stops, and within two or three days the network of tiny blood vessels begins to shrink in size. This deprives the surrounding tissues of both support and nourishment. The whole structure gradually becomes detached, and small pieces of the lining start to shed. Within a few hours, some of the weakened blood vessels open, first only a few at a time, then steadily increasing in number. Each tiny vessel empties its droplets. This is how the flow begins and soon increases.

The total amount of the average menstrual flow is about two to three ounces, which is only about four to six tablespoonsful of liquid. The amount may vary. For some women it may be less than an ounce; for others it may be much more.

There is no medical reason for avoiding intercourse during any part of the menstrual period. No ill effect occurs from penetration by the penis, nor is menstrual blood harmful. However, if either husband or wife consider intercourse at this time distasteful, it should be avoided.

How Menstruation Stops.   As soon as each area of old lining has been shed and washed away, the blood vessels in that patch return to their original size, become sealed, and are again closed. Finally, only a few patches remain to be cleared away. The flow then tapers off and ends. What had recently been a deep red spongy lining is now reduced to a smooth pink surface ready for new growth. This is how menstruation begins and then ends, for the first time in adolescence, and each time thereafter until menopause.

The Number of Days of Menstruation.   The amount of growth and shedding tends to be so consistent that most women find they always menstruate the same number of days. The average number of days is four to five. For some women it may be only two or three; for others, equally normal, it may be a full week or more.

The Number of Days Between Menstrual Periods.   The number of days between one menstruation and the next is generally far less consistent than the number of days of flow. The average length of the cycle from Day 1 of menstruation to Day 1 of the next cycle is between twenty-six and thirty-two days. This is only an average, however, and almost all women occasionally vary at least two to three days; many vary by several days from time to time, and some are always quite irregular. The important thing to remember is that throughout the years each woman establishes her own general menstrual pattern, which becomes normal for her but which should be expected to have some unpredictable variations at times.

A girl or woman menstruating should be free to engage in any activity she would pursue if she were not menstruating. Specifically, she may go horseback riding, swimming, engage in any strenuous games, or she may wash her hair or bathe. A study done at the University of Illinois in 1960 proved conclusively that a significant amount of water does not enter the vagina when a woman sits in a bathtub or when swimming.

One of the early signs of cancer of the cervix may be bleeding after sexual intercourse. One of the signs of cancer of the uterus may be spotting of small amounts of blood between menstrual periods. If any unusual bleeding occurs, you should report to your doctor for an examination as soon as the bleeding has been stopped for forty-eight hours.

It is important for you to wait the forty-eight hours so the cervix and vagina will not be obscured by blood and so a Pap smear or a uterine aspiration may be done. If there are fresh blood cells present a Pap smear cannot be taken. Do not take a vaginal douche before this examination.

Conception and Pregnancy

Fertilization takes place in the shelter of a mother's oviduct, which is the tube that leads from the ovary to the womb. This is the meeting ground for the successful union of the female egg and the male sperm cell.

Egg and Sperm. The round egg of the female is the largest single human cell, yet it is smaller than a dot (·). The male spermatozoon, *sperm* for short, is similar in shape to a comma. It is much smaller than the egg, so much smaller that 2,500 would be needed to cover this comma (,)—and all the sperm needed to repopulate the world could be fitted into an aspirin tablet! The egg is so much larger because it is laden with food to sustain a growing embryo in its first few days. The relatively cumbersome egg is motionless, but the sperm is agile. With the lashing of its hair-fine tail, a sperm cell can propel itself ahead about one inch in eight minutes, which, for its size, is a much better speed than an athlete can match. At that speed, a sperm may reach the egg in an hour to an hour and a half. By way of comparison, an athlete would have to run 70 miles per hour for 250 miles to approximate the speed and distance traveled by a sperm.

Egg and sperm come together from opposite directions. At ovulation the immobile egg is thrust out of the ovary in a gently rising spring of fluids and is swept up by the fingerlike fringes (fimbria) into the oviduct opening. It must be fertilized within twenty-four hours or it will disintegrate.

During this time, the egg will be in the upper part of the oviduct. The sperm may be waiting there or may arrive after the egg. Sperm cells have a longer life span than the egg. They stay alive and vigorous for two to three days and, according to some evidence, may survive even much longer. Sperm do not have to arrive exactly at the time of ovulation. They may arrive some hours before it, or after it, providing an approximate total of at least four to five days in each monthly cycle during which conception can occur. (*See* Figure VI, page 60.)

In sexual intercourse the spermatozoa are ejected in a somewhat forceful fine stream that normally aims at the narrow entrance of the cervix and

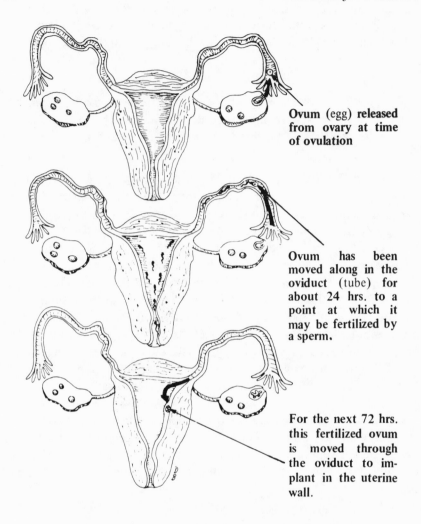

Ovum (egg) released from ovary at time of ovulation

Ovum has been moved along in the oviduct (tube) for about 24 hrs. to a point at which it may be fertilized by a sperm.

For the next 72 hrs. this fertilized ovum is moved through the oviduct to implant in the uterine wall.

Figure VI

The process of fertilization

When the egg is thrust out of the ovary in a gently rising spring of fluids, it is swept up by the finger-like fringes (fimbria) of the oviduct and carried along the tube. Note that the oviduct is not attached to the ovary in any way; yet the tiny egg is miraculously carried into the place where it can meet the sperm.

some immediately progress through it. Their entry is made easy at the time of ovulation by the fact that the normally dense mucus that protects the entrance to the cervix is much thinner and more fluid.

How Is the Egg Fertilized? Most of the millions of sperm fail to make the journey from the vagina to the oviduct. A few dozen do, but only one will fertilize the egg. It is thought that the first sperm that happens to reach and penetrate the egg may create a chemical change that shuts out all others.

The one sperm that enters the egg loses its tail, which is absorbed, and its head alone proceeds on through the food-rich substance of the egg. This one tiny sperm carries the father's threads of inheritance to the egg's center, where the mother's threads of inheritance lie. These threads are called chromosomes and they contain thousands of smaller units called genes that will specify the genetic, or inherited, characteristics of the new life. Among the threads of inheritance carried solely by the father will be the sex of the baby. Whether it is to be a boy or a girl will be determined solely by the sperm which carried the sex determining chromosome. In a few hours, the threads of inheritance of the two parents become knitted together. The egg is now fertilized. In a few hours the fertilized egg begins to divide and goes on to become a cluster of bubblelike cells.

The Nine Months of Pregnancy. The cell cluster drifts down the oviduct and into the uterus in about four days. By the end of the first week, it comes to rest on one spot, usually in the upper part of the uterus. There it clings and takes root. A few blood vessels may be broken open during this process called implantation, or nesting.

The nesting cluster finds nourishment in the lining of the uterus, which was prepared in the menstrual cycle. Toward the end of the second week, the cluster begins to form an embryo. This is about the time when menstruation would ordinarily have occurred. Further production of pituitary hormones is inhibited. This suppresses ovulation, maintains the endometrium (lining of the uterus), and postpones menstruation for the duration of pregnancy.

Outwardly, the first two months of pregnancy bring few changes to the mother. The breasts will enlarge and begin to be tender as a result of the change in the hormone level. In some women, morning sickness may occur temporarily. After about the twenty-seventh day, the placenta, the so-called afterbirth which is attached to the lining of the uterus and is linked to the embryo by the umbilical cord, starts a variety of functions necessary to maintain the pregnancy. One of these functions is the production of the hormone chorionic gonadotropin. Since chorionic gonadotropin rises to a high level for a short period of time, its detection in urine serves as a test for pregnancy. This test can be performed in a few minutes with a high degree of accuracy. Another function of the placenta is the production of progesterone. It takes over this important job as the ovary stops secreting progesterone. This hormone from the placenta is vitally important in maintaining the pregnant uterus and equally important in preventing the ovaries from developing another mature egg.

Quietly, a tremendous change is taking place. The whole embryo is being formed in this time from head to toe. Every feature and every vital organ is started in the first two months. The heart begins to beat on about the twenty-second day, but it is still so small that it cannot be heard easily for another four to five months. At the end of the first month the embryo is only about the size of a small pea. By the end of the second month it is about one inch long and so fragile that it is nearly weightless. At this time the embryo is called the fetus. It can move its arms and legs, turn the head, open and close the mouth, and swallow.

In the last three months of pregnancy the reproductive system becomes stretched to its limits in size and in capacity for supplying nourishment. The baby gains about five to six additional pounds, some of it as a padding of fat. From the maternal bloodstream the baby also accumulates essential immunities to diseases. Its lungs mature, and its strength and coordination improve.

The uterus has now increased its capacity about five hundred times. In the ninth month a poorly understood chemical reaction causes profound changes in the great muscles of the uterus. This is labor. In the first stage of labor the muscles of the uterus exert a force of about fifty pounds per square inch to push the baby out through the cervix. The narrow opening of the cervix gradually expands to let the baby's head and body pass through. Next the baby stretches the walls of the vagina and reaches the light of day.

Birth

Birth is remarkable—all the more so because the reproductive organs, having performed an enormous task, very soon return to their former size and functions. Within about a month they are ready to begin again. The first ovulation after delivery is likely to occur about this time. Although nursing may hasten the return of the reproductive organs to their original size and may delay menstruation, it will not prevent ovulation as many people believe. Therefore, conception can occur before the first menstrual period after delivery. Most often the first period occurs about six weeks after delivery. The new mother should be returning to her physician for her "six weeks" examination, and unless she wishes another pregnancy to follow very soon, it is essential to discuss with her physician the method of conception control she wishes to use. Even if she has used a method at an earlier time, it must now be reevaluated in view of the physical changes of childbearing.

Immediately after the birth of a baby, the mother has a great drop in her estrogen level, for she has almost no estrogen production from the ovaries. During pregnancy all the estrogen was being produced by the placenta, which is no longer present. Some new mothers may feel very depressed after the birth of their baby because of this lowered estrogen level. Also, if the baby continues to nurse for several months, the mother may develop thinning of the vaginal lining, since nursing also suppresses the production of estrogen. (This thin vaginal lining is like senile vaginitis older women develop in the menopause years.) A thin vaginal lining causes painful intercourse and requires the use of estrogen cream placed up inside the vagina once or twice daily until a few weeks after the baby stops nursing. During this time if there is any discomfort, do not neglect to use ample K-Y Jelly or some other lubricant before every sexual union.

Male Reproductive Organs

To aid in understanding the anatomy of the male sex organs, please refer to the accompanying drawings. (*See* Figures VII and VIII, pages 64, 65.) There are three basic male sex organs:

1. The *penis* (pē ' nĭs), with its glands and tissues

2. The *testicles* (tĕs ' tĭ kls), also called the gonads or sex glands

3. The *prostate gland* (prŏs ' tāt), and *seminal vesicles*

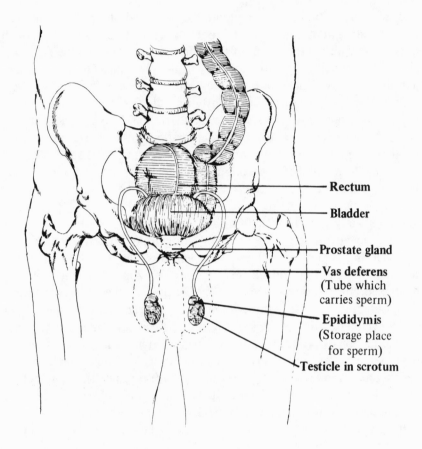

Rectum

Bladder

Prostate gland

Vas deferens
(Tube which
carries sperm)

Epididymis
(Storage place
for sperm)

Testicle in scrotum

Figure VII

Front view of male reproductive system

In this view of the reproductive organs, notice the relationship
between them, paying special attention to the vas deferens and
its ready accessibility in the scrotum. It can be squeezed between
thumb and fingers and feels like a small cord. A section of it
may be easily removed in the vasectomy operation.

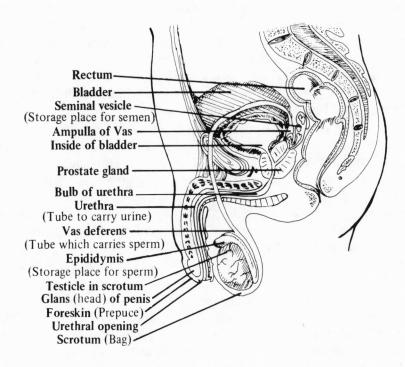

Rectum
Bladder
Seminal vesicle
(Storage place for semen)
Ampulla of Vas
Inside of bladder

Prostate gland

Bulb of urethra
Urethra
(Tube to carry urine)
Vas deferens
(Tube which carries sperm)
Epididymis
(Storage place for sperm)
Testicle in scrotum
Glans (head) of penis
Foreskin (Prepuce)
Urethral opening
Scrotum (Bag)

Figure VIII

Side view of male reproductive system

Semen (the seminal fluid) is manufactured and stored in the prostate gland and the seminal vesicles where contractions force it into the urethra at the time of ejaculation. As you can see, any enlargement (hypertrophy) of the prostate gland may interfere with the flow of urine from the bladder.

Penis

The most obvious fact about the penis is that it can be distended with blood under mental or physical stimulus so that it becomes stiff or erect. The penis is made up of three columns of spongy erectile tissue—the middle one containing the urethra. The head of the penis is called the glans and is very sensitive to touch. The glans contains many nerve endings which help build orgasmic tensions during sexual contact.

At birth the glans is covered by a fold of skin called the prepuce or foreskin. The foreskin requires special care to keep clean and to prevent accumulation of a greasy secretion called smegma. If the foreskin is too tight, it may interfere with erection and intercourse. For these reasons, the practice of circumcision shortly after birth has grown in popularity as a hygienic measure. Circumcision is the cutting off of enough foreskin to leave the glans exposed.

For many years some peoples, by custom or religion, have practiced circumcision. It is interesting to note that this is the only surgical operation mentioned in the Bible. About 4000 years ago God commanded that the operation be done on the eighth day after birth. Yet, it is only in the last twenty years that this has been found to be the very day when blood-clotting and infection-preventing factors are the most favorable they will ever be in a baby's life. Today, however, the timing of this operation is not as critical, because we have modern surgical instruments and drugs with which to avoid and control infection.

The urethra is a small tube which carries the urine from the bladder through the prostate gland and the penis. The outside opening of the urethra is called the meatus. The urethra is lubricated by secretions from glands near the base of the penis. These secretions help the sperm to make their way out.

The length of the unstimulated or flaccid penis varies greatly, but the erect penis is usually from five to seven inches long. Smaller or larger dimensions are not abnormal, however. Practically all the sexually stimulating sensations take place in the glans of the penis for the male and in the clitoris for the female. So, length of the penis has little to do with stimulation of the wife, or with satisfaction for the husband. Contrary to popular belief, there is more chance for a wife to feel discomfort and a lack of satisfaction from too large a penis than from one which is too small. However, a penis of any length is capable of providing full satisfaction. During erection the rim of the glans becomes a little harder than the tip and increases female excitement by friction. So, in the past it has been assumed that an extra benefit of circumcision was to permit the rim to stand out more from the adjacent tissue of the penis. However, recent research proves there is no difference in sexual sensation whether the male is uncircumcised or circumcised.

Testicles

The two testicles are carried in the scrotum, or bag, which is divided into a double sac. Each testicle, or testis, is about the size and shape of the nutlike female ovary—one inch by one inch by one-half inch. Each testicle consists of a mass of long tubes which are continually manufacturing sperm cells. The sperm move from the testicle into the epididymis, which is another network of tubes covering one side of each testicle. The sperm are then carried to the seminal vesicles in two long tubes called the vas deferens. Each tube is about eighteen inches long and takes a roundabout course through the inside of the pelvis.

In performing a vasectomy for sterilization of the husband, a one to two-inch section of each vas deferens is removed. (*See* Figure IX, page 68.) This surgery can usually be done under a local anesthetic in your doctor's office, and you should be able to return to your regular job within two days. This operation will not affect your sex life—it just stops the sperm from going from the testicles to the seminal vesicles. Men want to know what happens to the sperm after a vasectomy. The tiny sperm cells are still produced, but they dissolve and are absorbed in the epididymis.

Be very sure you do not wish to have any more children before having a vasectomy, because a vasectomy operation is usually irreversible. However, in some medical centers a highly specialized type of reparative surgery is being performed. The surgeon must use special operating microscopes, very delicate instruments, and tiny sutures to reunite the cut ends of the vas deferens. This is a very long and tedious operation which costs several hundred dollars, and even with such delicate surgical technique there is no assurance of a return of fertility.

It must be noted that the failure to maintain sterility from a vasectomy operation is related to the length of the section of the vas which was removed. If a two-inch section is removed, there will be very few fail-

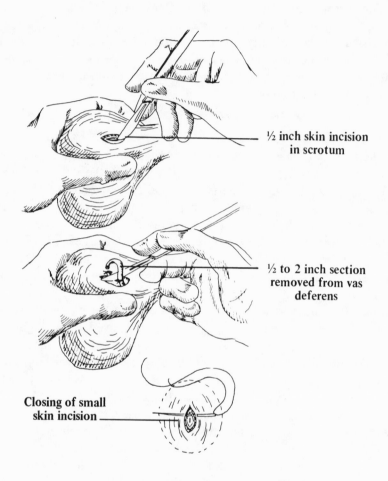

½ inch skin incision
in scrotum

½ to 2 inch section
removed from vas
deferens

Closing of small
skin incision

Figure IX

Diagram of vasectomy operation

A small amount of local anesthetic is injected into the skin of the
scrotum before the incision is made. This operation is usually
performed in the physician's office.

ures; but if only a very short segment is removed, the failure rate will be somewhat higher. This failure is possible because scar tissue may form between the cut ends, and a new pathway may develop through the scar tissue.

If you elect to have a vasectomy operation but still harbor some thought that you might later desire to have reparative surgery to enable you to father a child, be sure to communicate your desire to your surgeon, so that he will remove only a very short section of the vas deferens.

Just before it enters the prostate, the vas from each testicle broadens out into the ampulla, or semen reservoir. Opening off these two reservoirs are the seminal vesicles, which consist of two large pouches above and behind the prostate gland. When the seminal vesicles fill with secretions, there is stimulation of the reflex nervous system. Sex desire in the male, therefore, arises periodically, spontaneously, and consciously, and is localized in the sex organs.

While in the seminal vesicles, the sperm cells are joined by a lubricating secretion that helps them do their next job—swimming. Other similar secretions are added to make up the final seminal fluid, which is then stored until ejaculation. During sexual climax (ejaculation), the fluid is forced from the seminal vesicles through small tubes that meet in the ejaculatory duct just before entering the base of the penis. The muscular contractions that take place in the surrounding pelvic muscles and in the prostate gland suddenly force the seminal fluid past the base of the penis, then on through the urethral canal, and out the meatus. This fluid is projected forcefully and may travel a distance of twelve to twenty-four inches if unhindered. The contraction of the prostate gland provides much of the pleasant sensation of sexual climax.

Prostate

The prostate gland is a very important gland similar in size and shape to a large walnut. The prostate surrounds the urinary passage right at the base of the bladder and is located between the urinary bladder and the base of the penis. After some men are in their fifties and sixties, the prostate may gradually grow to a size which blocks the flow of urine from the bladder. This necessitates a prostatectomy—that is, removal of the prostate gland. After this operation, the semen at the time of ejaculation often goes into the bladder instead of going through the penis and into the vagina. This does not greatly alter the physical sensation of a man's orgasm, but special instructions from a urologist will have to be followed if a pregnancy is desired.

If there are repeated episodes of failure to ejaculate, especially following prolonged arousal periods, there may be some injury to the prostate gland which may lead to a condition known as prostatitis. (This also occurs in men not yet married but engaged in prolonged petting.) Symptoms include low back pain, pelvic pressure, urethral discharge, and slight pain while urinating. While the urine is usually free of infection, the prostate is enlarged, sometimes tense and very tender.

The man who has sexual relations on a "feast or famine" schedule (such as a salesman or truck driver who is away from home at regular intervals) often develops a congested prostate during the famine periods. When he has frequent intercourse, the prostate keeps on producing seminal fluid to keep pace. But when the sexual activity stops, the prostate is still working at the same rate to produce fluid, and soon the resulting congestion causes prostatitis.

This requires prescription medication and twice-weekly prostatic massage by a physician placing his index finger into the rectum and applying firm pressure to the usually swollen and tender prostate gland. This treatment may be required for three to eight weeks.

Most husbands with prostatitis are glad to hear that increased frequency of sexual intercourse is a distinct help in speeding recovery and preventing further trouble. However, some men have told me their wives *never did believe* they were given this information as a part of their medical prescription. Now I hand each prostatitis patient a *written* prescription containing this advice!

Semen

Just past the prostate are the two openings of glands which secrete mucus to lubricate the urinary canal for easy movement of the semen during ejaculation. Some of this lubricating fluid may escape from the penis during the erection before climax (or orgasm). The fluid, with the secretions from the female vagina, helps provide easier entry of the penis into the vagina. This oozing during excitement is natural and beneficial and does not mean that semen is being "lost," nor is it a sign of sexual weakness or venereal disease. However, you must be careful, as there may be enough sperm in this small amount of lubricating fluid to produce a pregnancy. This is one of the reasons the withdrawing of the penis from the vagina just before ejaculation is not an effective means of birth control.

It is generally agreed that there are from 250 to 500 million sperm cells present in the half-teaspoonful of semen ejaculated during a normal sexual contact after three or four days' abstinence. An estimated count of fewer than 60 million per cubic centimeter is usually considered to be inadequate for fertilization. But, some recent work has indicated that conception is still possible with as little as 20 million sperm per cubic centimeter. A low sperm count requires some simple but specialized procedures to make the best use of the sperm that are produced. Fertility procedures are discussed in chapter 11.

The semen is primarily protein, similar to egg white, and is not dirty or unsanitary despite its distinctive odor. We do not advise a vaginal douche after intercourse, but a few women may produce a large amount of lubricating fluid, which mixed with the semen produces enough discharge material to be objectionable. These women may occasionally desire to douche. For some it may seem easier just to insert a tampon a few minutes after intercourse.

Male/Female Similarities

As we conclude this section on physiology, it is interesting to realize that the female and the male sexual organs develop out of the same structures. The most obvious of these similar or "homologous" structures are the clitoris and the penis. The clitoris repeats—reduced and modified—the chief elements of the male penis. The spongy tissues of the clitoris that engorge with blood are similar to the glans penis with its numerous nerve endings and great sensitivity. The muscles at the base of the penis are repeated in the pubococcygeus (P.C.) muscles surrounding the vagina. The female "major lips" are the counterpart of the male scrotum. In some degree, the meeting of the outer folds of the inner lips over the clitoris corresponds to the foreskin over the glans of the penis.

It is clear that the sexual organs, both male and female, have other functions besides the propagation of the race. Even before the human being is fully mature and able to reproduce, the sexual glands (the ovaries in the female and the testes in the male) have begun their work of making a woman or making a man, as they manufacture some of the hormones which encourage and control the rate of physical development, mental growth, and psychological maturation.

Now as we go on to discuss the processes involved in sexual response, you will appreciate the reason for this detailed study of the anatomy of the sex organs.

5

One Flesh:

The Techniques of Lovemaking

Within the intimacy of their marriage and in the privacy of their bedroom, a man and woman gradually learn the meaning of the Genesis pronouncement: "They shall be one flesh."

Please note that this is a *learning* process, with husband and wife progressively discovering how to provide pleasure for each other. They begin with some explicit information (the more the better); then with growing delight they find out by experience and application of information just how to make love and impart joy to their mate.

Several hindrances have blocked this learning process in the past. First of all, young couples were brainwashed by the romantic novels and movies which suggested that "it all comes naturally." Then many people have been defensive about their knowledge and skills as lovers, feeling that they must pretend to know it all or else admit to personal deficiencies.

Today, more and more Christian couples are seeking counsel in the area of the sex relationship because they do not want to depend on the trial-and-error process, which may or may not lead to satisfaction. They are beginning to understand that the Lord has designed blessing and pleasure for them, and they do not want to miss out on it. The first reason for marriage, according to Scripture, is companionship: "It is not good that man should be alone." God designed marriage to keep people from being alone. If in any area—spiritually, psychologically, or physically—

73

the man and wife are not one with each other, then they are *alone* in that part of their life. Some Christian couples may be beautifully related in one mind and one spirit; they may have a good marriage in many ways. But their marriage remains incomplete and unfulfilled if they do not know how to please each other in the intimacy of their physical relationship.

Detailed how-to-do-it books on sex are readily available these days so that a great deal of information is at hand. Unfortunately these publications are sometimes medically erroneous, often crude and distasteful in presentation. Worst of all, they miss the mark for the Christian reader who realizes that much more than a selfish seeking of physical sensation is involved. The discerning lover approaches the experience knowing that the keenest pleasure comes from the exquisite joy of pleasing the beloved.

The act of love is experienced as a single ecstatic episode by the two involved, but medically it can be analyzed and divided into four phases which reflect the physical changes that occur. Before we discuss them, let us consider the physical environment most conducive to a meaningful relationship. Most important is your need for privacy. In considering buying or building a home you should pay close attention to having your bedroom and bath as isolated as possible from other rooms. Every master bedroom needs a good lock, controlled from the inside of course. Every child should be trained not to disturb his mother and daddy when their bedroom door is locked. If a couple is to concentrate totally on each other (which is necessary for maximum enjoyment), they must be assured of protection from intrusion. Under no circumstance should you allow a child to sleep in the room with you, except perhaps a new baby for the first six months or less.

The question of lighting in the bedroom should also be considered. Some wives are better able to abandon themselves to maximum expression of enjoyment by having sexual intercourse in a room with very little or no light. However, the husband is greatly stimulated by seeing his wife's body and watching her responsive movements and expressions of delight. For this reason, you may wish to vary your settings between darkness and very soft light, even candlelight. Remember that the mystery of the body enhances the lovemaking experience.

Phase I : Arousal

This time of sexual stimulation often called foreplay can be delightful for both if the husband realizes that his tender skill at this point will prepare his wife for the love act itself. Most women like to be wooed and won. Let the man indicate by the way he approaches his wife that he is demonstrating his love for her, not claiming sex as his right. Husband, I caution you not to be hurried, crude, rude, mechanical, or impatient!

Before beginning sex play, a bath will show one's mate how important the event of physical unity is. When married, bathing at night before getting into bed makes good sense. When during the day will one be in as intimate contact with anyone as during the night when sleeping together? Bathing and shaving at night will show love, respect, and an anticipation of touching and closeness.

Relaxed love play begins with kissing, embracing, petting, and fondling. The most effective touching for both man and wife in the early part of sex play is a gentle caressing of *all* the body. *All* means including everything and excluding nothing. Do not touch only those areas that seem directly related to excitement. Your partner may enjoy caresses on the inner thighs, the lower back and buttocks, the earlobes, the back of the neck, or. . . . Caressing of varied areas shows an interest in the whole person. As Solomon said, "Thou art all fair, my love; there is no spot in thee" (Song of Solomon 4:7). And his wife, the Shulamite maid, said of Solomon, "He is altogether lovely. This is my beloved, and this is my friend. . ." (Song of Solomon 5:16).

Caressing each other should *never* be hurried. Only lust and self-gratification are done in haste. Take the time to fully enjoy each other! It is important to understand the timing of lovemaking. There should be a gradual building and intensifying of emotions and sensations. Do not stop or let up the stimulation once begun, but continue in an ever-increasing arousal. During this phase a long hug or any period of stillness will serve to slow or reverse sexual tensions, especially for the wife. The movement of thigh against thigh, her breasts against his chest, and stroking each other's back and shoulders are much more exciting than a clinging hug. Each part of the body moving against the spouse's body will greatly heighten sexual tensions.

The union of marriage frees the couple to enjoy their bodies in whatever ways are most pleasing, provided that both are being pleased. Without restrictions (other than selfish acts which hurt the partner or evoke distaste), the couple should feel free to experiment and to "know" each other in the most intimate sense possible. Love involves close bodily contact and the pleasure of seeing, touching, and enjoying with all the senses. Let this be your guide in love play.

The very first sign of sexual arousal in the husband is erection of the penis, and this occurs within a few seconds after being triggered by caressing, a stimulating sight, or an erotic train of thought. After only one or two minutes if effective stimulation continues, he progresses into the second phase, which is the time of increasing excitement. If this excitement phase can be prolonged for ten to twenty minutes or more, a much more overwhelming orgasm will result. The wife may need to occasionally fondle the shaft of the penis to keep the erection full for this length of time.

In the wife, lubrication of the vagina may take place within ten seconds of sexual arousal. This corresponds to erection of the penis in the male, but it is only a beginning sign of arousal for the woman and does not signify readiness for intercourse.

Phase II: Time of Increasing Excitement

Following the arousal phase a gradual and not well-defined transition into the time of increasing excitement occurs. After the preliminary period of stroking other parts of the body, the husband may enjoy fondling his wife's breasts, and his caresses and kisses there may be very exciting for her as well. From fondling he should move to slightly more intense caressing as her excitement heightens. The later stages of manual stimulation of the wife's breasts should be on the nipple area and should also be graduated with soft kissing and touching. The nipple becomes more firm and will stand out from the breast; then as excitement increases, the nipple may appear to be somewhat hidden by the swelling of surrounding tissues. Since the nipple becomes more sensitive with touching, this surrounding engorgement helps protect the nipple from excessive stimulation.

A gentle caressing of the genitalia will greatly increase sexual excitement at this point. Be creative and imaginative rather than rough, blundering, or predictable in your approach. Remember, always, that stirring the imagination helps bring about the most response in both men and women.

Oral sex (mouth to genital) is a matter which concerns only the husband and wife involved. If both of you enjoy it and find it pleasant, then it may properly fit into your lovemaking practices. If either partner has any hesitancy about it, however, it will add little to the pleasure of the relationship and should be discontinued.

One goal of lovemaking is to fill a treasure trove of memories with delightful love experiences which will quicken the responses during your next times together.

The Song of Solomon (2:6 and 8:3) describes a position ideal for intensified love play. "Let his left hand be under my head and his right hand embrace me," the bride says. (The Hebrew word translated *embrace* usually means to embrace lovingly, to fondle or stimulate with gentle stroking.) In this position the wife lies on her back with her legs extended, comfortably separated, and her husband lies down on her right side, placing his left arm under her neck. In this way he can kiss her lips, neck, and breasts, and at the same time his right hand is free to fondle her genitals.

As excitement continues to rise, the clitoris swells and the labia minora (inner lips) at the entrance to the vagina become two or three times enlarged. This swelling of the outer vagina reduces the opening to effectively grip the penis. Other responses may be tensing of muscles, increased pulse rate, and sometimes a general flush of the skin (similar to a measles rash) especially over the upper abdomen and the chest. There may be almost spastic contraction of some sets of muscles in the face, chest, abdomen, and buttocks. Voluntary tightening of the sphincter muscle which holds the anus closed and some voluntary contractions of muscles of the buttocks may help heighten sexual tension.

In the past it was thought that the wife should restrain her natural urges while the husband should release himself as soon as possible. Quite the opposite is true. The wife should learn to let go and be as free as possible, while the man must learn to control the timing of his response.

The wife should concentrate on her physical feelings so that she can communicate her stages of progress to her husband with looks, touches, and loving verbal communication. This is recommended so that he can perceive the level of her sexual excitement and properly time his lovemaking. One of the most common sources of sexual unhappiness is the failure of women to tell their husbands frankly and clearly what stimulates them and when they are ready for a particular stimulation.

While the husband's caresses of the wife's genitalia are vital in bringing on the wife's orgasm, the wife's caresses of the husband's genitals do not usually speed up the male orgasm. While excitement has been building in both partners, when the wife actually touches the husband's genitals it is soothing and comforting to him.

The wife's very light gentle caressing should center around the inner thighs, the scrotum, and the top surface of the penile shaft. Stimulation here will help maintain the husband's erection. Touching of the scrotum should be very light, since the scrotum is quite pressure sensitive. Fondling the head of the penis and the frenulum on the underside of the penile shaft will greatly increase the husband's excitement but may also trigger ejaculation more quickly than desired. By fondling and lovingly touching her husband's genitals, the wife soothes him and quiets his responses while her own excitement builds.

The clitoris, rather than the vagina, is the center of feminine response, and its stimulation will produce orgasm in almost all women. Increase of arousal will come from manual play at and alongside the clitoris more often than from placing fingers in the vagina. As excitement progresses in the wife, the shaft of the clitoris will enlarge and become firmer. The firm clitoris usually can be felt at the peak of the surrounding lips above the vagina. Before sexual excitement it is very difficult even to find the shaft of the clitoris, and it is important to note that in 30 percent of women there is no discernable enlargement of the clitoris during sexual arousal.

If the husband has given his wife enough stimulation to build excitement, some natural lubrication may be brought to the outside from within the vagina. A well-lubricated clitoris will be much more sexually responsive to the husband's touch. If the wife does not produce enough natural lubricant, some K-Y Jelly may be used to lubricate the clitoris and vaginal opening. (Be careful to warm the K-Y Jelly by holding the tube in warm running water before you go to bed.) Applying the lubrication can in itself be exciting to the wife as it shows her husband's tender care for her. Trying to stimulate a dry clitoris or inserting a penis into a dry, tense vagina indicates lack of understanding or selfishness and should be avoided. Clitoral sensitivity in some women increases to the point where direct stimulation may become unpleasant (too much!) or even irritating. Therefore, movement of the husband's fingers should be directed to the area immediately around the clitoris. A consistent and persistent movement of the husband's fingers alongside the shaft of the clitoris is usually most effective in heightening her excitement.

When the labia minora on each side of the vaginal opening engorge or swell, the husband receives an important clue as to how far along his wife is in her arousal. These inner lips may so engorge that they protrude beyond the outer lips. The husband can only judge when this occurs by learning how to detect it with the tips of his fingers as he stimulates his wife. This swelling of the inner lips is the most easily observable physical sign telling the husband that his wife is ready for insertion of the penis.

Husband, although this is one sign of readiness, never insert the penis until the wife signals you to do so. Always insert the penis in the most gentle way and never follow immediately with vigorous thrusting, as this usually decreases arousal in the woman. Most couples have found that it is very useful for the wife to insert the penis. She knows exactly where it should go. This will avoid interruption at this very important time. Even after entrance of the penis, she may still need light caressing of the clitoris to increase excitement to orgasm. It is estimated that 30 percent of women regularly require manual stimulation of the clitoris to achieve orgasm.

Positioning of the couple's bodies should suit their own individuality. There need be no set patterns, although early in marriage, the bride, not having had her tissues stretched from childbearing, may find that some angles of penile insertion will cause discomfort. After several children have been born, the tissues around the vagina will be stretched, and the wife will then be more comfortable in varied positions. Remember, changing of positions may restore interest and encourage excitement, but these new positions must be comfortable and pleasing for both husband and wife. It is worth noting that the right rhythm of movement is just as important as the right position in attaining a satisfactory response for both partners.

The **male-above position** is by far the most commonly used and gives the husband freedom of movement plus greatest control of strength and rapidity of thrusting. Many couples consider this the most satisfying of all positions. The wife lies on her back with legs extended, comfortably separated. The husband lies on top of her, supporting some of his weight on arms or elbows, his legs inside hers. After insertion of the penis her legs may be moved farther apart, closer together, inside his, or wrapped around his legs or up over his body.

To assume the **female-above position** the husband lies on his back while the wife straddles his body and leans forward. *She* inserts the penis at about a 45-degree angle and moves back on the shaft rather than sitting down on it. She then assumes whatever posture is most stimulating and comfortable to her. This position allows the wife by her movements to control the exact timing and degree of thrusting that affords her the most sexual response. The placement of each partner's legs will govern deeper or less deep penetration of the penis, depending on what is preferred. The female-above position gives the husband access to her breasts. He also has free use of his hands to better stimulate the clitoris if necessary while they are joined in sexual intercourse. This position is often advantageous for a large husband and a small wife and is sometimes more comfortable as the abdomen enlarges during pregnancy.

Starting intercourse in the female-above position, the *lateral*, or *side-by-side position* is assumed by the wife leaning forward and shifting her body slightly to the right, placing her right leg between her husband's legs. Her left leg is then flexed over his right leg. Advantages of the lateral position are that each partner has at least one hand free for fondling and caressing. Each is free to thrust or rotate hips. Neither has to support weight with hands and legs, and neither is being ''pinned'' by the body weight of the other.

The *male-behind position* seldom is used but may be tried on occasion and may also be used during late pregnancy. Both husband and wife lie on their sides facing the same direction with the husband back of the wife. The penis is placed into the vagina from the rear. Disadvantages are that the penis does not contact the clitoris and the couple cannot kiss during intercourse. This position leaves the husband's hands free to caress the body and breasts and stimulate the clitoris.

We have described the basic positions here. Others are given in chapter 12 in the discussion of sex during pregnancy. By all means feel free to explore the pleasure of other positions that you imagine would be exciting for you and, of course, acceptable to your mate.

It should be understood that the size of the penis has nothing to do with how much either partner enjoys intercourse, as only the outer two inches of the vagina contain tissue which is stimulated by pressure on the inside. Many men think deep penetration of the penis gives their wife greater stimulation, when it is actually better contact with the clitoris that will increase her stimulation to the point of orgasm.

Phase III: Orgasm

The man's orgasm consists of involuntary muscle tension and contractions, with sensation centered specifically in the penis, prostate, and seminal vesicles. His orgasm is complete when he has expelled the semen.

Husbands, there are five things which will increase the physical intensity and pleasure of your orgasm: (1) Wait at least twenty-four hours after previous orgasm to allow the body to store a larger volume of seminal fluid; (2) Lengthen the foreplay and excitement period so that the penis can remain erect about twenty minutes; (3) Increase your imagination factor by seeing and feeling your wife's ecstatic response to your knowledgeable, skillful, physical stimulation which brings her to the point of maximum physical pleasure; (4) Voluntarily contract your anal sphincter muscles during your orgasm; (5) Increase the force of thrusting while your orgasm is in progress.

The wife's orgasm consists of a series of rhythmic contractions of the muscles of the lower vagina (called the P.C. muscle group). She can increase the intensity of the physical sensations by voluntarily strengthening her muscle contractions and adding her own pelvic movements to his as she abandons herself to seeking release. When her physical movements, response to his stimulation, and mental concentration blend into a total reaching for satisfaction, she too will experience this wonderful physical sensation designed by the Creator. The climax is exactly that—a high point of feeling best described as ecstasy.

During these few seconds of intense sensation known as orgasm, both husband and wife experience various muscular responses, even facial grimaces. As they both move in rhythm they usually grasp one another tightly. Men and women are sometimes unaware of their extreme muscular exertions during orgasm, but it is not uncommon the next day to notice muscular aches, particularly in the back and thighs.

As soon as the husband finishes ejaculation, he should immediately begin manual stimulation of his wife's clitoris so that she can have repeated orgasms. This is the way the woman is designed! She should not have to ask for this, as the whole sex relationship is a striving to please each other. This means it is not desirable to change pace by having to ask for something for one's self. It should be the natural desire of the husband to provide every pleasure he knows of, and the wife may be intensely pleased by this continuing stimulation.

While arriving at orgasm at the same time may be a goal for lovers, it is not nearly as important as aiming at mutual enjoyment. Some begin to experience simultaneous orgasms as they come to understand each other more intimately. What does matter is that both partners be fully satisfied in each sexual encounter.

Time is all-essential. Take time to thoroughly arouse each other physically. Take time to ensure the wife's orgasm and the husband's controlled, full response. Finally, after intercourse, take time to express your love and appreciation for each other.

Phase IV: Relaxation

Picture this final phase according to the poetic term one doctor has given it—*afterglow*. After intercourse is over, the fires of passion and pleasure settle down to a lovely, quiet glow. Let this be a time when the husband shows tenderness toward his wife with hugs, kisses, and love pats. The couple should continue to express their appreciation as they lie close in each other's arms and just enjoy each other's presence. This ensures a smooth transition to complete relaxation together. It may be as long as thirty minutes before all the physical signs of arousal are gone, and in a younger man it may be as long as an hour before the erection completely disappears.

You will find a unique joy in using all the skill you possess to bring pleasure to your marriage partner. In fact, every physical union should be an exciting contest to see which partner can outplease the other. The husband should be the world's greatest authority on how to please his wife. And the wife should be able to say as joyously as the bride in Song of Solomon—"I am my beloved's, and his desire is toward me" (7:10).

6

Tortoise and the Hare: Solutions to Common Problems

Couples hoping for good sexual adjustment in marriage are dismayed early in their relationship when instead of pleasure they find problems in their lovemaking. There are two basic problems, and virtually every couple encounters one or both of them, at least at the beginning. These are not as complex or as hard to solve as one might think. The real problem lies in the fact that these difficulties are often ignored or excused until poor adjustment becomes an accepted, expected part of the sexual relationship.

Here are typical complaints heard in my office:

From a young woman: "His lovemaking just doesn't last long enough for me!"

From a weary husband: "It takes my wife forty-five minutes to come to a climax if at all. I'm so tired after a hard day at work. . .it's hardly worth the effort."

From the mother of six: "There must be more to sex than babies and hangups! I almost never get any enjoyment out of our physical relationship."

From the older man: "I'd like to be a better husband. But our sex life was so unsatisfying to my wife for so many years that she is completely indifferent now. I know it's not too late to learn. . .if only she wanted to learn with me."

I can assure any couple that it is not too late to develop a good sex relationship. As we consider these basic problems I will show you proved techniques to overcome them, almost wonder-working in their simplicity and effectiveness. Some effort will be required along with the desire to reach sexual adjustment.

If you recall the pokey tortoise and the excessively speedy hare of Aesop's fable, you will be able to picture both problems. The tortoise represents most often, although not always, the wife. By this I mean that a large proportion of women take a longer time to reach orgasm than do their husbands. Correspondingly, a large proportion of men are like the hare. They reach orgasm too quickly, before their wives are sexually fulfilled.

God in His great wisdom did create most women to become more slowly aroused than men. This prevents the sex act from being just a mechanical process; instead, it is an opportunity to learn to interact—to give and to receive reciprocal attention in a way that both partners can be satisfied.

Before husband and wife can learn how consciously to adapt to each other's need, two conditions may become evident: orgasmic dysfunction in the woman and/or premature ejaculation in the man. This means that some women are very slow to reach orgasm, rarely reach orgasm, or may never have had an orgasm. In the case of the men, premature ejaculation means the inability to control ejaculation for a sufficient length of time to satisfy the wife. When the latter condition is solved, the wife often has no difficulty in reaching sexual release.

It usually is possible for couples to solve these problem conditions with the use of some simple physical exercises which they can do together. In the process of learning how to consciously slow down or speed up, they also develop valuable nonverbal communication processes and come to realize their dependence upon each other. The result: a more harmonious marriage in every aspect.

Some readers who do not suffer from premature ejaculation or orgasmic dysfunction may be tempted to pass over the remainder of this chapter. Let me encourage you to read on. The exercises I will suggest can improve *any* marriage. Every couple I have dealt with has had something to learn, either in control or in better use of what God had provided. Most have something to learn in the area of timing, adjustment, or rate of response. While the husband learns to control his speedy responses, the wife learns to intensify excitement so that she can respond to him more quickly and more fully.

Premature Ejaculation

Because premature ejaculation can be the primary cause of the woman's orgasmic dysfunction, we will discuss ejaculatory control first. Specifically, the term describes the husband who ejaculates before entering his wife's vagina, or ejaculates immediately after entry. It also refers to the husband's inability to control ejaculation for a sufficient length of time during intravaginal containment to satisfy his wife in at least 50 percent of their times of sexual intercourse. In other words, the husband arrives at ejaculation *before he wishes to do so*.

One main cause of premature ejaculation is poor learning experience at the beginning of marriage. A new husband who has built up great tension through the period of courtship and engagement may well ejaculate when he takes his wife in his arms on their wedding night, and for many nights thereafter. Some men mistakenly feel that a quick release is a sign of masculinity. Thus they never realize the need to learn to control the timing of their ejaculation so that they can experience the joy and oneness that comes with consistently bringing the wife to orgasm during intercourse.

The problem of premature ejaculation is occasionally established from sexual experiences before marriage. Heavy petting with stimulation to ejaculation can form a hurried pattern of lovemaking. Premarital intercourse instills guilt about the sex act itself, and in such furtive acts there is the constant pressure to "get it over with" before discovery. This pattern of hurried ejaculation will usually continue after marriage until the husband realizes that there is a need to change. A good sexual adjustment is always a learned experience. It does not come naturally.

The main difficulty with premature ejaculation is that it does not give full sexual satisfaction to the wife. When this problem persists, the pattern of the marriage is somewhat predictable. The wife feels that she is being inconsiderately used, that her husband is only concerned with his own pleasure and has no real appreciation of her sexual needs. She is left without a means of physical release and builds an increasing level of resentment at being *used* sexually rather than *loved* sexually. In the usual course of events, after a period of years, husband and wife both withdraw from some of the commitment of marriage; the man doubts his masculinity and the wife loses her confidence as a woman. As the man becomes more and more anxious about his failure to satisfy his wife, he may even lose his ability to maintain an erection. This is called impotence. A quiet but hostile marriage without sex may endure.

Another problem of premature ejaculation is that a "satisfied" husband has a tendency to discontinue his physical attentions to his wife after his orgasm. Not only is the wife denied the feeling of sexual release in orgasm, but she may also have acute and chronic physical pain stemming from congestion of her pelvic organs, engorged with blood that is normally released with orgasm. Thus the wife is frustrated when he falls asleep at her side. He is snoring and she is fuming!

An occasional premature ejaculation can occur in the most controlled of men, especially when there is sexual union after the husband and wife have been apart for a number of days. If this is the case, the husband should immediately begin to use his fingers to gently stimulate his wife's clitoris, since his penis will no longer have the firmness necessary to stimulate her to orgasm. Thus the wife is assured of her husband's concern for her complete sexual fulfillment.

The need to prolong erection and delay ejaculation is a problem that has been around for a long time. Until recently, a man's only solutions were to concentrate on something not associated with sex (sometimes difficult to accomplish while in the sex act), to take tranquilizers, or to apply some type of anesthetic cream or a sheath to the penis. None of these so-called solutions is completely effective or satisfactory.

Sometimes the husband tries to solve the problem by using manual stimulation to bring the wife to a very high degree of sexual tension just before insertion of the penis. A disadvantage of this technique is that the wife is often so desperate to have her orgasm that her frantic thrusting produces almost instant ejaculation by her husband, while she still needs more time.

Many other factors may add up to produce an unsatisfactory sex relationship. Since the husband can be relieved by ejaculation, he may not see the need to change for his wife's sake. Researchers have found that many such men are selfish and do not consider themselves inadequate lovers, but blame their wives for not being sexy enough. The husband may assume that his wife also enjoys the relationship as it is; or he may assume that her slower response is all her problem. The wife may further complicate the situation by faking orgasm and faking enjoyment of sex in order to please her husband. The false idea that pleasure in sex is unnecessary for the woman, as well as the belief of some wives that sex is strictly a duty, has contributed greatly to the misery of the tortoise-hare relationship.

Recognizing and admitting that a problem exists is half the battle won. Too many couples simply go on for years accepting premature ejaculation, not even realizing that *they* have a problem. A few couples would rather not contemplate a change where they have failed so often in the past. It becomes easier and easier to remain in the same old rut rather than get on the road to a solution.

The husband's problem is easier to remedy than the woman's; so, men, you no longer have to be the hare. With the methods we will discuss, you can slow down to be of greater help to your wife, and at the same time gain more satisfaction and confidence in yourself!

Although it is essential at the beginning for the husband to admit that he has the problem of premature ejaculation, both he and his wife should view this as a "couple" difficulty requiring "couple" cooperation to find the solution. Husband and wife need to covenant together to follow through a relatively short program of practical exercises that will definitely help in a matter of a few weeks. In the course of these procedures they will learn the technique of *squeeze control*, in which squeeze pressure is applied to the erect penis. This technique causes no pain, since most of the pain-sensitive areas in the male genitals are in the testicles rather than the penis, but it does make the husband lose his urge to ejaculate, and often he loses some erection momentarily. (The squeeze-control procedure was presented by Masters and Johnson at the Reproductive Biology Research Foundation in St. Louis, where Gaye and I studied at one of their post-graduate workshops for counselors and educators in the field of human sexual function and dysfunction. I am giving you this as I have adapted it in my medical practice.)

The wife must understand that the squeeze control technique is not effective if done by the husband on himself. She must be involved! With her full cooperation and willingness to learn and apply certain basic principles, and with warm personal involvement expressed openly, this troublesome marital problem can be solved. Much greater sexual pleasure will be the reward for both partners.

Since the premature ejaculation problem may have been present for a long time, no couple should expect an immediate solution. It will take time to form new response patterns. Practice sessions of at least twenty minutes duration should be carried out lovingly and leisurely with little attention given to the clock. It is important not to skip practice sessions, and they should never be shortened to less than twenty minutes unless an ejaculation accidentally occurs.

During the course of this program, one can get so caught up with avoiding orgasm that tension builds. Remember, there is no harm in an orgasm by mistake. Nevertheless, strictly avoid orgasm as a goal. Special objectives are given for each phase of the program. But always, learning physical communication and building sensitive understanding is of key importance. Each session should be a time of pleasure and enjoyment for both partners, never hurried and never tedious.

Repeat a phase at your practice sessions until you have mastered the objectives of that particular phase. *This means that you may spend a number of practice sessions on one phase before you are ready to go on to the next.* These sessions may take place on a daily basis or at two-or three-day intervals. I suggest that the total duration of the first four phases not exceed four weeks, as prolonging this time tends to lead to boredom.

Premature Ejaculation Control Exercises

Phase I

You may both be so "gun-shy" from the husband's quick sexual release that you have been avoiding touching as much as possible. You need to take the focus off orgasm and timing and concentrate on improving nonverbal physical communication without seeking to reach orgasm. Objective of this phase: *To improve physical communication and learn to appreciate physical closeness with your mate.*

1. Spend time touching and fondling each other.
2. Do those things which physically please your mate, such as a scalp massage or stroking the back or neck, etc.
3. Avoid directly stimulating genital areas.
4. Do not have intercourse, but focus on improving physical communication with your mate.
5. Learn to appreciate and enjoy physical closeness.
6. Follow this procedure for at least the first two sessions.

Phase II

Objective of this phase: *For the husband to learn to recognize the physical sensation that comes just before ejaculation so that he is able to communicate to his wife the best time to apply the squeeze.*

During this session it is vitally important that the husband concentrate completely on his own sensations. He is to block out all other thoughts so that he will become keenly aware of the feeling that comes just prior to ejaculation. It may help if he closes his eyes. As soon as the husband feels he is nearing the point of ejaculation he is to indicate this to his wife by some predetermined word or signal. She is then to quickly use the squeeze technique. This phase should be repeated during the daily practice sessions until the husband can consistently recognize the sensation that occurs just before ejaculation. (*See* Figure X, page 90.)

1. The wife is to sit with her back against the headboard of the bed, with her legs spread comfortably apart.

2. The husband is to lie on his back, with his head toward the foot of the bed.

3. The husband positions his pelvis between his wife's legs, with his genitals close to hers. With knees bent, his feet are to be placed outside her thighs (near her buttocks).

4. The wife now lovingly and gently caresses the man's genitals, paying special attention to the underside of the shaft or the head of the penis, or wherever her husband directs, to encourage him to attain an erection.

5. As soon as the husband achieves full erection, the wife will begin the squeeze technique. She places her thumb on the underside of the penis, about one-half inch below the slit opening just where the shaft ends and the head begins. She then places the first two fingers of that hand on the opposite side of the penis, with one finger above the ridge and one finger below the ridge which distinguishes the head from the shaft.

6. She then squeezes her thumb and two fingers together with very hard pressure for about four seconds.

7. She then quickly releases the pressure.

8. After fifteen to thirty seconds, she manipulates him to full erection again and repeats the squeeze. The husband should inform his wife by word or subtle signals when he feels she needs to repeat the squeeze to delay his orgasm.

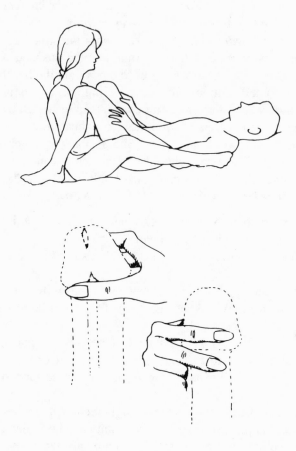

Figure X

Positioning for premature ejaculation
training session using squeeze control

9. Repeat this procedure every four to five minutes for the entire twenty-minute session.

10. The husband may prefer to have a lubricant such as K-Y Jelly applied to his penis in order to more closely experience the sensations felt during sexual intercourse.

11. Do not have intercourse or insert the penis into the vagina.

12. At the end of the session, stimulation should be continued to ejaculation.

13. It will be desirable for the husband to use manual stimulation of the wife's clitoris to give her sexual release *after* each practice session.

Phase III

Objective of this phase: *For the erect penis to remain almost motionless in the vagina for fifteen to twenty minutes before ejaculation.*

1. The husband lies on his back, and the wife stimulates him to an erection.

2. When he feels he is nearing the point of ejaculation, he signals his wife and she is to quickly use the squeeze technique.

3. She should repeat the stimulation almost to ejaculation and then squeeze the penis. This should be done several times.

4. Then the wife straddles the husband in a sitting position. Leaning forward at about a 45-degree angle, she very gently and slowly inserts the erect penis into the well-lubricated vagina, then moves backward comfortably onto the shaft, not just sitting down on it.

5. She remains motionless, giving her husband a chance to achieve control. If the husband loses his erection while the penis is in the vagina, the wife should raise her body and manually restimulate him to erection.

6. If the husband becomes aware that he is nearing the point of ejaculation, he should indicate this to his wife so that she can raise her body and repeat the squeeze procedure. Then she gently reinserts the penis.

7. Husband and wife should be able to maintain this position with the erect penis almost motionless in the vagina for fifteen to twenty minutes before ejaculation.

Phase IV

Remember, it is important to wait at least one day before beginning a new phase. The objective of this phase: *To be able to keep the erect penis in the vagina with very gentle movements for about twenty minutes before ejaculation.*

1. Spend some time in loving foreplay.
2. Again assume the position of the wife straddling the husband and leaning forward.
3. The husband is to begin thrusting slightly, thus learning to tolerate gradually increasing amounts of movement of the penis in the vagina.
4. This gentle thrusting should be continued for fifteen to twenty minutes before ejaculation. Use the squeeze technique if necessary.
5. When this phase is mastered, the husband may now ejaculate with the penis in the vagina, but he is to continue concentrating on his own sensations until each practice session is over and he has ejaculated. Then he is to take time to manually bring his wife to orgasm. (Remember, this is still a training session.)

Phase V

The objective of this phase: *To learn how to have comfortable sexual intercourse in the side-to-side (lateral) position.* (This position gives better control of movements by both husband and wife and allows the husband the best ejaculatory control.)

1. Spend some time in loving foreplay.
2. Again assume the position of the wife straddling the husband and leaning forward.
3. Place a pillow under the husband's head and another one along his left side.
4. The wife brings her right leg to a straight position between his legs. She leaves her left leg on the outer side of his body.
5. At the same time, the husband brings his left leg out from his body, placing it flat on the bed, with knee bent.
6. The wife is to shift her entire body slightly to the right, while leaning forward with her left breast at the level of his left breast. She will now be partially supported by the pillow at her husband's left side. Additional comfort is achieved by another pillow for her head and shoulders.

7. It will take several practice sessions to learn to change easily into this side-to-side position and arrange the arms and legs in the most comfortable manner. (Once learned, this position is used by many couples most of the time.)

8. While in the side-to-side position, the thrusting should be gentle so that the penis can remain in the vagina for twenty minutes before ejaculation.

Establishing Lasting Ejaculatory Control

1. Use the squeeze technique at least once a week for the next six months.

2. Once each month practice the squeeze technique for an entire twenty-minute session.

3. Good ejaculatory control is usually attained in three to six weeks.

4. Within six to twelve months the husband should be able to be consistently quite active in intercourse for ten to twenty minutes without ejaculation.

5. Complete control is attained when the husband does not have his orgasm until he chooses.

Prolonged emphasis on controlling orgasm in these practice sessions may sometimes cause a husband to have a temporary lack of ability to keep an erection. Do not be dismayed. It is just this portion of the husband's body demanding a brief rest.

As you read this detailed list of instructions for the practice sessions, the process may seem to be rather tedious. But any couple who recognize that premature ejaculation plays some part in their lack of maximum sexual fulfillment will find that a few weeks of mutual effort and discipline will lead to far greater sexual pleasure for the rest of their lives. It is a fact that few men possess the ability to delay their ejaculation as long as they would like. These training sessions using the squeeze technique procedure can result in heightened pleasure for any couple desiring a better sexual relationship.

During the squeeze technique sessions, the wife may discover that she is beginning to experience some new and pleasurable feelings. She begins to feel more sexual arousal. She may even experience her very first orgasm. Even if she has been able to reach orgasm before, she may now begin to enjoy multiple orgasms.

The Pubococcygeus (P.C.) Muscles

Just as the husband has shown an effort of sacrifice and love in gaining complete ejaculatory control, so the wife can also contribute to the relationship by attaining full control and strength in the muscles which surround the lower third of her vagina in order to experience a much more intense sexual stimulation.

Before we discuss this important muscle group (pū bō kŏk sĭj ′ ē ŭs) I should point out that most of what researchers have called "orgasmic dysfunction" in women is not caused by a physical dysfunction. Most failure in achieving orgasm is related to the wife's attitudes and thoughts. The next chapter will discuss this in detail. However, by undertaking these specific exercises to build up certain important muscles, the wife can usually begin to participate in and enjoy sex. These physical exercises, along with the restructuring of attitudes about sex, have had great success in treating "orgasmic dysfunction" in women.

Exercising to strengthen the P.C. muscles can be undertaken effectively though other factors still may inhibit the wife's orgasm. While it is always desirable to treat the entire person—body, mind, and spirit—still, an improvement in just one area will improve the whole person in some degree. In fact, it may be the one "missing link" which will trigger a satisfying sexual response. Even if the husband is uncommunicative and unwilling to share in the total improvement of sexual relations in marriage, the strengthening and toning of the P.C. muscles is done with exercises that the wife can perform by herself. This can be an encouragement to him and shows him that she really desires to help improve their sexual relationship.

Other important benefits of improved P.C. muscle control are:

1. Improvement of support of pelvic organs.
2. Improvement of urinary control.
3. Reduced extent of childbirth injuries to the mother.
4. Shortening of length of time in labor and delivery.
5. Increased safety for the baby during the birth process.
6. More effective natural childbirth. (The exercises are included in the YWCA classes for natural childbirth and in the International Childbirth Education Association programs of instruction, as well as the Lamaze Method.)

In the early 1940s, Dr. Arnold H. Kegel, a surgeon and professor of gynecology at the University of Southern California School of Medicine, made a discovery about women who had trouble controlling their urine flow when coughing, laughing, or sneezing. It was found that this problem, referred to as *"urinary stress incontinence,"* could be helped by exercising the pelvic muscle group called the *pubococcygeus muscles* or P.C. muscles. In medical school anatomy books they are called the *levator ani muscles.*

The P.C. muscles are located above the legs and extend from the pubic bone to the coccyx in the back. The P.C. muscles are like a sling and form the floor of the pelvis, also supporting and surrounding the outer one-third of the vagina, the neck of the bladder, and part of the rectum. (*See* Figure XI, page 96). Dr. Kegel found that repeating specific exercises strengthens the P.C. muscles, with resultant stoppage and control of urinary stress incontinence. The exercises he prescribed to strengthen the P.C. muscles are called the Kegel exercises.

Further study by Dr. Kegel revealed that fewer than one in three women have adequate P.C. muscle tone. However, women who have poor muscle tone do not necessarily have urinary leakage. The strength of the P.C. muscles seems relatively unrelated to general muscular development of the woman. Since the P.C. is suspended between two solid nonmoving bony structures, its strength is unaffected by the use of other muscles. Therefore, a female athlete can have poor P.C. musculature, and a weak, inactive woman may have strong P.C. musculature.

The stretching that occurs during childbirth weakens the P.C. muscles. Uncontrolled urinary leakage most often appears after a woman has borne children, since much of the support for the bladder comes from the P.C. muscles. The urethra, or urinary passage, penetrates and is also supported by the P.C. muscles. When these muscles are weakened, poor urinary control often results. Under ordinary circumstances, even weak muscles can hold back urine; but under a stress like a sneeze, laugh, or cough, urine is sometimes allowed to escape. In less than two months most of the patients who followed Dr. Kegel's exercises were able to control their urine flow. Today these exercises are a standard technique for learning to establish urine control, and when these muscles are strengthened, there often is no need for surgical repair. For many patients, the Kegel exercises strengthen and build much better pelvic support than a surgical operation.

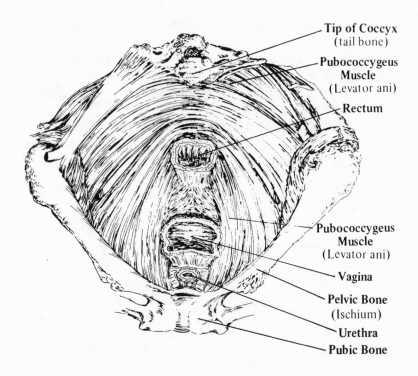

Tip of Coccyx
(tail bone)

Pubococcygeus
Muscle
(Levator ani)

Rectum

Pubococcygeus
Muscle
(Levator ani)

Vagina

Pelvic Bone
(Ischium)

Urethra

Pubic Bone

Figure XI

**Pubococcygeus muscles viewed from below
looking from front to back**

Note the extent of the P.C. muscles as they form a primary part of the
support for the reproductive organs, bladder, and rectum. Weakness of
the P.C. can result in chronic pelvic discomfort or leakage of urine.
Refer back to Figure I in Chapter Four in order to better visualize the
location of the P.C. muscles.

One patient reported to Dr. Kegel that for the first time in fifteen years of marriage she had orgasm in intercourse and suggested this welcome event might be connected with the exercises she had been doing. After following the exercise program, other women also volunteered the information that they experienced more consistent orgasm during intercourse, or had orgasm for the first time.

Dr. Kegel finally concluded that strengthened P.C. muscles resulted in increased sexual satisfaction. This information, though new to our culture, had been observed by primitive and oriental peoples as well as other cultures who also noted the lessening of sexual satisfaction after childbirth. Certain "secret" sex practices in some primitive cultures depend on controlling and strengthening these muscles around the vagina.

Since Kegel's early efforts, research has revealed that sexual stimulation in the woman's vagina is much more related to *pressure sensitivity* than to *frictional sensitivity*. This stands to reason because the P.C. muscle group is well supplied with pressure-sensitive nerve endings (called proprioceptive nerves) which do *not* respond to light touch or light friction. Thus, a strengthening and tightening of the P.C. muscle group around the outer one-third of the vagina can produce much more pressure sensitivity for the woman during intercourse.

These pressure-sensitive nerve endings of the P.C. muscles are actually around but *outside* the vagina. A *firm* squeezing pressure upon the penis within the vagina is needed to give greater sexual stimulation. A vagina which makes poor contact with the penis affords little sexual stimulation for the wife. It has been found that a larger object introduced into the vagina does not help increase sexual sensitivity, since sensitivity depends on *contraction* of the muscles—not stretching. Therefore, the size of the penis has no relationship to sensitivity for the wife. However, when the vagina is tightened to a firm channel by a strong P.C., thrusting of the male penis will also press and push the P.C. and give more satisfying stimulation to the wife. More stimulation results in reflex contraction of the vagina, which is part of the pattern that leads to orgasm for the woman.

In a woman who does not experience orgasm during sex, the P.C. muscle exercises can contribute to providing relief of pelvic congestion and muscular tension which is a very frequent cause of low back pain. The exercises are easy and not fatiguing—in fact, if you tire while doing them, you are not exercising the right muscles.

Some women can easily contract the P.C. muscles when they first learn of their existence and may experience orgasm for the first time when they learn to use these muscles during intercourse. However, if the muscles are weak (as they are in so many women), action will have to be added to knowledge. The woman must learn an exercise which can help her to both strengthen and control the P.C. muscles.

The P.C. Exercises

The following instructions are directed to wives who want to experience the benefits of these exercises. I will explain them to you as if you were a patient in my office.

You might have difficulty locating the P.C. muscles at first. Without instruction it is more likely that only the weaker, external muscles around the vaginal opening will be contracted. This error will be seen by a pursing or tightening of the vaginal opening only. Being told that the P.C. muscle group is more internal often causes the woman to contract muscles of the lower back, abdomen, and thighs. These muscles are not linked to the P.C., and contracting these may cause fatigue. The P.C. muscle exercise should be fairly effortless, though it may take some patience and concentration at first. After the exercise is initially learned, it's almost as easy as shutting your eyelid.

Since one of the functions of the P.C. muscles is to stop the flow of urine, it can be said that the P.C. muscles have been contracted if urination is interrupted. However, the less important external muscles can also shut off the urine flow; so the simplest method to determine if the muscles contract is to attempt to stop urine flow with the knees spread. In the sitting position on the commode, with knees widely separated (about two feet apart), allow the flow of urine, and then attempt to stop the flow without moving the knees. In nearly all women, this procedure exercises the P.C. muscles. Once you feel what it is like to correctly contract the P.C., you can do the exercise any time. The stoppage of urine flow during urination can then be used once in a while as a check to make sure you are contracting the right muscles.

Another way to tell if the P.C. muscles are being contracted is to see if the perineum rises. The perineum is the area between the anus and the vaginal opening. Use a mirror to observe the rise of the perineum or place one finger about an inch and a half inside the vagina and feel the muscle contract. When there is good P.C. muscle control, you should be able to squeeze this one finger very firmly.

After learning precisely how to contract the P.C., a program of exercising is begun. Start with five to ten contractions upon waking and every time you urinate. Hold each contraction for two seconds. When control of the P.C. muscles is improved, you should be able to release as little as a teaspoon of urine at a time. The contractions should be easier than when first attempted.

In approximately four days, when you have confidence you are contracting the P.C. muscles, increase exercising to ten contractions about six times per day. If each contraction takes two seconds, the total time involved will be only two minutes per day. Over a four to six-week period, gradually increase to 300 contractions per day, which should require no more than a total of ten minutes per day. Better urine control and some sexual improvement may be occurring by now. About four more weeks (or a total of ten weeks) should complete the program. More planned exercise probably should not be necessary, since strong and well-developed P.C. muscles will keep the involuntary urine flow under control. Occasionally check to see whether you can still tightly squeeze one finger in the vagina.

Sexual activity also helps strengthen the P.C. muscles. Women are advised to start voluntary contractions of the P.C. during foreplay in order to heighten sexual tension before the penis is inserted. This helps condition the P.C. for involuntary contractions later in orgasm, and it also helps firm up the vaginal walls. By consciously contracting these muscles the wife can have an earlier response and more intense pleasure. In the final spasms of each orgasm, the P.C. contracts by itself, involuntarily, four to ten times at intervals of four-fifths of a second. After these independent contractions, there is a tremendous feeling of release and lessening of tension which signals that the wife's orgasm is over.

Most nerve endings in the body are sensitive to light touch; the nerve endings in the P.C. muscles, however, are sensitive to pressure instead. Obviously the skillful use of the P.C. muscles during intercourse is included in the design of God to give increased sexual stimulation to the woman.

P.C. muscle contraction can also provide your husband more pleasurable sensations during intercourse. Also, when you develop voluntary control and when there is loving, verbal communication between the two of you, you can learn exactly when to contract the P.C. muscles to give him the maximum stimulation just before and during his orgasm.

You can see how important your involvement is and how necessary your helpful participation is in sex play, both for your husband's benefit and your own. Remember, as we have said elsewhere, that the vagina is *not* a passive receptacle for the penis. Picture it as an active, involved organ during sex. The role of the vagina was described fifty years ago by Dr. Th. H. Van de Velde in *Ideal Marriage*: "The working of the . . . muscles . . . is an apparatus for gripping and rubbing the male sexual organ . . . by pressure and friction, to ensure this orgasm."

Ask yourself how good your P.C. muscle control is right now. The muscle should be able to grip the penis as tightly as a clenched fist.

Almost every woman can significantly heighten her sexual adequacy through understanding the Kegel exercises to condition, strengthen, and achieve voluntary control of the P.C. muscles. And some men have found more intense physical sensation in orgasm after strengthening their own corresponding pelvic muscles.

The few weeks of exercises for ten or fifteen minutes per day add up to very little time or trouble, and yet the rewards are great for both the wife and her husband. They enjoy more satisfying sex, and the benefits are lifelong; it all adds up to an experience that should be well worth the effort.

Here is a case history for your encouragement from Dr. Tim LaHaye's *The Act of Marriage*:

> One such case, a mother of five and married almost twenty-five years said, "Dr. LaHaye, it all seems so unnatural to me. If God wanted those vaginal muscles strong enough for me to get more sensation during lovemaking, He would have made them that way." I explained to her that He did originally, but her five births and natural aging process had so relaxed them, they were of little help to her and the older she grew, the more she would need them toned up through exercise.
>
> Quite reluctantly, she went home to try, but she admitted she had little faith it would work. Fortunately, she did her exercises diligently and as she reported later: "Within one month I experienced sensations I had never felt before. Within five weeks my husband, who had been

having a little trouble maintaining an erection, had noticed how much more exciting our love life became. Now we both think our next twenty-five years of lovemaking will be more exciting than the first twenty-five.''

Along with the exercise, here are further suggestions for the woman learning to experience orgasm: The ability to build sexual tension or excitement after actual introduction of the penis must be actively sought and learned. You should keep anticipation and desire foremost in your mind, surrender to your own natural drives, and build emotional excitement as well as physical stimulation until your tension climaxes in release. Many women have found that they are able to reach a climax more quickly if they also tense the muscles of their legs, thighs, and lower abdomen while mentally concentrating on their own sensations, until they have orgasm.

Vigorous thrusting as soon as the male organ enters the vagina usually guarantees the wife's sensation will be blurred, and that excitement will actually decline.

A gentle introduction of the penis will almost always better meet the wife's needs. Both partners may wish to develop some mutually pleasing movements with the penis fully inserted—perhaps side-to-side movements, rocking motions, or hip movements which help take some of the thrust away from the upper end of the vagina and direct the pressure to the more responsive lower vagina which is surrounded by the P.C. muscles. The husband should be very sensitive and responsive to his wife's movements.

The art of lovemaking involves an enjoyment of each phase of the experience, seeking every pleasurable sensation, anticipating but not hurrying toward release. As you learn this art together, your ''tortoise and hare'' problems will diminish and disappear!

7

For the Preorgasmic Wife: Fulfillment Ahead

This part of *Intended for Pleasure* is written especially for the woman who seldom or never reaches sexual release during intercourse.

I want to speak very directly with you who up to this time have been unable to enter into the sexual pleasure God designed for every wife. In the past you would have been called frigid—a word that seems to denote an icy personality, unfeeling and self-contained. And yet you know yourself to be a warm and loving woman. It's just that you haven't been able to experience the thrills and excitement you've read about. You love your husband, and you want all there is from marriage. Perhaps both of you are feeling discouraged because it hurts too much to go on failing, so why keep trying? Why not be content just with loving each other and settling for what must surely be second best? I assure you that you do not have to miss out on the *pleasure* of sex with your husband.

Nor do you have to think of yourself as *frigid*. Today we reserve the expression *frigid* for a woman who finds the sex act distasteful, even offensive. The more accurate term for the woman who has never reached a sexual climax is *preorgasmic*—which implies fulfillment ahead; delayed, *but only for a time*.

Now, failure to achieve a sexual response may have stirred up feelings of frustration, self-doubt, and inadequacy in both you and your husband. This is an understandable reaction. When these feelings come from sincere attempts to express love to your mate, the wound goes very deep as you begin to sense failure in the very area in which you most want to

103

succeed. Yet, never forget that the warmth of your love does exist. It is the ability to express and receive this warmth physically which has become blocked by memories of previous failures coupled with a lack of sexual knowledge.

Your problem may be rooted in the past, even before marriage, but psychological causes can seldom be exactly pinpointed, and the only purpose served by seeking something in your past is to find someone or something on which to place the blame.

The mature approach for the Christian couple is to realize that no matter what the cause, *God is able to meet your need in any situation.* You and your husband can start right where you are by asking God to raise your level of love and sexual interest for each other, and then both of you can enter into a mutual, loving cooperation in following some simple instructions.

Before I give you an effective (and pleasant) procedure—a series of training sessions—to solve this problem, there are principles to be underscored.

First, no matter which of you may seem to be the most at fault, both you and your husband will have to make a fresh start, as if you were just now getting married. Quit worrying about who might be at fault. This is not the issue. It is only important to discover how both of you can experience more pleasure in your sexual relationship.

So give each other a chance to make love without demand or criticism. This is not a time to keep score, but a time to practice and learn together without anxiety. This will be a period when you realize both of you have much to learn: you learning to receive, and he learning to give unselfishly.

Your goal will be to build up memories of pleasurable sexual feelings. When those are combined with some new experiences and a realization of your husband's loving desire to give you sexual pleasure, this will increase the number of signals to the brain which can build up to an uninhibited sexual response.

Second, I want you to understand yourself. *Desire* is your ally. If you desire to have an orgasm because you know it is your right, your provision from God, and because you want to keenly enjoy the most intimate times with your husband, then there is no reason why you cannot experience an orgasm. It will come.

But it will not come as a result of your exerting your will power.
Certain things must happen within your body as you are sufficiently
stimulated, and orgasm will be the result. You can never work it up by
trying. Yet, intense concentration is an important key. I hope that does
not sound like a contradiction. The concentration must be upon your own
feelings, your own sensations, your own desires, as you move with them
and let them take you where they will.

Third, beware of factors which can break your concentration and keep
you from sexual release. What will break your concentration? You may
find yourself becoming a spectator at your own lovemaking, critically
watching yourself to see if you are "performing satisfactorily." Self-
consciousness will interrupt your enjoyment and turn off desire which
may be only just beginning.

Or you may find yourself concentrating on your husband's reactions.
You may starting worrying. "He must be getting tired. . . . This isn't
much fun for him. . . . I'm sure he wishes he had married someone more
sexy. . . ." And by that time another facet of self-consciousness will
have spoiled all sensual delight just as it was beginning to flower.

A third interruption in concentration may come from guilt feelings of a
rather interesting variety. You may have overcome psychological hurdles
in thinking of sex as a "bad thing," for you now realize it is God-created
and God-ordained. But as you concentrate on your own wonderful new
sensations and look forward to a release of tensions, suddenly the thought
comes: *I should be trying to please my husband. It's wrong just trying to
please myself.* And again desire is aborted.

Let me give you true and sensible thoughts with which to program your
mind before you go into lovemaking:

1. In these "training sessions" there is no need to judge yourself, for
nothing at all will be demanded of you. The atmosphere will be relaxed
and yet sensuous to permit *a natural unfolding* of the sexual response
which lies within you. *Natural* means that you force nothing, that you
pretend nothing. It can be one of the most wonderful times of your life, as
a matter of fact, when nothing is required of you but to *let yourself* find
pleasure as it comes.

2. You may not realize how much your husband is going to enjoy
these training sessions! They are purely *pleasure-oriented.* Couples have

reported that their relationship became particularly close and romantic as they began to concentrate on each other strictly for pleasure, without pressure. As you cast off all self-consciousness you will become more sensual and more desirable to your husband.

3. As you learn to respond by concentrating on your sensations, you *are* learning to please your husband! You cannot imagine how devastating an indifferent response is to a man who tries time after time to arouse his wife with lovemaking. You also cannot imagine the ecstatic thrills which come to a man when he sees his wife responding totally, enjoying every moment of their time together with a lovely abandonment.

Now as you go into these training sessions your husband will have the opportunity to show you his love as he temporarily defers total sexual gratification. You will show him your trust as you put yourself in his hands and risk being completely vulnerable and honest in this relationship.

Your training sessions should be in a very private place with no chance of interruption. Of course you will both be very clean and as rested as possible. I suggest that your husband have a clean shave and trimmed, smooth fingernails. If his hands are even slightly rough, he should use a generous amount of hand cream or lotion to make his caresses more pleasing.

All caresses must be gentle, never harsh, brusque, or forced. If they are light, fleeting, and teasing in nature, they serve to arouse the imagination to a much greater degree.

You will both take off all your clothes, and your husband is to use his fingers and his hands to touch, massage, and fondle your body anywhere you lovingly direct him, while you just relax and become conscious of the pleasure gained from his care and caresses. At first, use a gentle trial-and-error method, maintaining very comfortable positions in bed, and avoid any thought of hurrying or any feeling of need to satisfy your husband, or any seeking for your own orgasm.

You should daily, for at least four days, repeat these unhurried relaxed times of receiving your husband's caresses for whatever period of time that gives you pleasure. For these times you may wish to actually avoid touching the genital or breast areas. You should now both be discovering the most sensitive areas of your body. You should also be aware that you have permission to freely express your pleasure in sexual feelings without regard at this time for your husband's sexual needs.

These few sessions in which you and your husband touch and caress each other unclothed will help to establish or reestablish a healthy climate of physical giving and pleasuring. The absence of actual intercourse during these sessions will help reduce tensions which have built up in former experiences of coitus.

Also, during this period you should learn to talk things over. You should begin to learn to anticipate the other's physical wants and needs. Remember, if your husband tries a particular form of caress on you, it would be a good idea for you to reciprocate. The idea that it might be pleasurable probably occurred to him because he would like the same caress returned!

You can begin touching your husband, and as you delight him spontaneously and without duty you may find your own pleasure increasing.

Up to this time, you should not have directed your husband's hands to your breasts and genital area, but now you must follow some detailed directions for maximum pleasurable sexual stimulation. Your husband is to place himself in a sitting position with his back comfortably resting against pillows at the headboard of the bed. With his legs widely separated, you are to sit between his legs with your back against his chest and your head resting comfortably on his shoulder, your legs spread apart and draped over his. This position allows him freedom of access for creative exploration of your entire body. You should encourage specific direction for this by placing your hand lightly on his hand, so you can show by slight increases in pressure or by gentle directional movement, the "where and how" of your desires at any particular moment. This will allow both of you to learn precise physical communication without the distractions of verbal request or detailed explanation. At this time you should direct his every movement, and he should absolutely refrain from any of his own ideas as to what may be stimulating to you.

Your husband may feel that he should now stroke the end of your clitoris, but this has been found to be too sensitive and tender an area. You will probably achieve much more pleasure by well-lubricated stimulation along the shaft or sides of the clitoris and around the upper part of the vaginal opening. Almost never is there pleasure in introduction of fingers deep into the vagina.

Often you will want him to just lightly stroke your neck, your earlobes, your breasts, your upper inner thighs, your buttocks, and then return to those most stimulating areas just above the clitoral area or around the vaginal opening.

There is no hurry, and you should not at this point be attempting to force yourself to reach an orgasm. These are pleasurable times which may extend over a period of several weeks when both you and your husband are lovingly discovering exactly what it is that excites you sexually, and learning to communicate with each other physically and verbally.

If at any time you feel that you are highly aroused sexually, you should try to continue increasing the intensity of the stimulation with his hand or your hand, until you experience the intensely exciting sensation of orgasm. The sensation is centered primarily in your pelvis. While you are learning with your husband you should have complete freedom to stimulate your own clitoris if you feel it is needed to produce your first few orgasms. This will help to start a pattern of response which will later make it much easier to experience orgasm in sexual intercourse. After you have had several orgasms by manual stimulation, you should begin having sexual intercourse in the female-above position. Then use whatever positions you desire.

Do not be concerned if your orgasm continues to come from manual stimulation of the clitoris. The idea that satisfaction for the wife should come from the penis in the vagina is only sometimes true. Your goal, now, is satisfaction given by a loving husband, and release of sexual tensions.

Also do not anxiously work toward simultaneous orgasm with your husband. This is wonderful when it happens, but has been far overemphasized in current literature. The point is: pleasure for both partners during the sexual relationship.

Remember skillful, gentle, appropriate stimulation of the clitoris and the nearby areas will almost always bring any wife to a higher level of desire and an experience of sexual release in orgasm.

You can see that the answer lies not just in collecting a group of new erotic techniques, but simply in learning to touch and enjoy each other, to communicate and discover how to please each other. As you learn to enjoy sex because of the wonderful sensations to body and the precious oneness with your mate, and not just because it is something that makes your husband happy—you will know fulfillment!

Some general observations should be made about physical conditions which produce pain during intercourse. Painful intercourse is called dyspareunia. This is a symptom, not a diagnosis; any woman who has pain or other difficulty with intercourse should have a thorough physical examination including pelvic and rectal examination. Since only a minority of doctors will ask a patient about the state of the sex life, you should never wait for the doctor to guess your difficulty. Just take a deep breath and tell him what is wrong. Be frank. Be specific. Be brief.

A common physical cause of pain is atrophic vaginitis, a thinning of the vaginal wall which is caused by a lack of female hormones, especially estrogen. This occurs when the amount of estrogen is reduced, or after surgical removal of the ovaries, or when the woman is in the menopause. This can easily be corrected by taking estrogen by injection, by mouth, or by applying an estrogen cream locally in the vagina.

Pain can also be caused by vaginismus, which is a term describing the involuntary action of the muscles of the vaginal entrance as they go into spasm when an attempt is made to insert the penis. This spasm may be so severe that even the little finger cannot be inserted into the vagina. This painful condition usually starts right at the time of the first attempt to have intercourse, but it may also occur at other times, such as after the birth of a baby, after a pelvic operation, or even at the time of beginning a second marriage.

Vaginismus can usually be easily eliminated by following this procedure: With the wife in position for pelvic examination on the examining table at the doctor's office, the husband is brought into the room and puts on a rubber glove. He is instructed to attempt to place one well-lubricated finger into the wife's vagina. This is to demonstrate to both husband and wife the severity of the spasm of these muscles around the outer one-third of the vagina. With concerned and loving cooperation, the husband is instructed in how to gently dilate or open the vaginal opening with some well-lubricated special metal dilators to be supplied by the doctor. These are called Hegar dilators. The larger-size dilator looks like a metal rod, a little larger than a fountain pen. When the larger size can be easily inserted, the wife should retain one of these in her vagina for several hours each night. I also use several progressively larger plastic vaginal dilators made for this purpose.

Well-lubricated sexual intercourse may now be started, usually without difficulty. However, for the next several weeks it may be necessary for the husband to use the dilator just before intercourse. It is very important that the husband actually do the dilating with the dilator as most vaginismus is caused by psychological problems, and his interested, loving cooperation is very important in the treatment.

An often overlooked cause of painful intercourse for the wife may follow childbirth in which there is a tear in the broad ligament which is one of the supporting structures at the side of the uterus. Pain is experienced on deep penetration of the penis, and it is very difficult for the doctor to find this injury. If you developed this pain about one or two months after you had a baby, be sure to ask your doctor to check for this tear. If he cannot find a cause for the pain, you should see a specialist who will be able to surgically repair this internal tear to provide relief.

Pelvic congestion is one of the most common causes of low back pain and pelvic pain and tenderness. During the time of increasing excitement all of the wife's pelvic structures become engorged with blood under a significant amount of pressure. If she proceeds to a strong orgasm, the involuntary muscular contractions close off the small arteries and open the venous system to produce draining of this pooled blood in a matter of minutes. This leaves a distinct, pleasantly overwhelming feeling and sensation of comfort and warmth in the pelvic area, followed by a rather complete feeling of relaxation.

However, each time the stimulated wife fails to reach orgasm, this represents some injury to the pelvic organs and to her emotions, often leaving her with nervousness, weakness, fatigue, and moderate to severe pelvic pain which may become chronic. This also may lead to chronic vaginal discharge or heavy or irregular menstrual bleeding. Unfortunately, many women undergo pelvic operations because of this pain. This repeated congestion may also contribute to significant enlargement of the uterus which may indicate to a doctor there is a disease which requires surgery. I suggest that none of you undergo surgery for pelvic pain until you have made every effort to learn how to achieve regular, full, sexual release by orgasm.

With any chronic pelvic symptoms, you should have regular pelvic examinations every six months to one year, as some physical condition could arise at any time which might require medical treatment.

Most cases of failure to attain orgasm that I have seen began with poor preparation for marriage, a frustrating and fearful honeymoon, followed by a prolonged period of disappointment, blundering, and boredom in marriage that conditioned the wife to feel there was no hope for fulfillment.

This situation was often aggravated by the wife's failure to understand that it is man's nature to be adventurous. When a man realizes his wife is not being satisfied, this inclination is increased even more as he attempts to please her. She begins to view his variety of approaches as distasteful, vulgar, or abnormal. Nothing will chill and remove the bright lustre of married love more quickly than a cool, silent, sullen, indifferent, or negative attitude toward the young husband's advances.

Applying the information given in this book, today's husband has the opportunity to become a skillful lover, one who can tenderly lead his wife into the richest pleasures of the sexual relationship—and remember: *every wife should be given the opportunity to experience sexual release in every intercourse.* The relationship may be very loving and warm, but this is not enough. Fulfillment ahead! This can be yours!

8

For the Impotent Husband: Fulfillment Again

George C., a physically strong, hard-working man of fifty-three, had desired intercourse five or six times a week during his married life—until recently. His wife complained that he no longer showed an interest in her. Upon questioning, she recalled that he had lost his erection a few weeks back, and they had terminated their lovemaking that night. They had never discussed it, but he had seemed indifferent since then. She also observed that he had taken on more responsibility in his job the past few months and showed an unaccustomed tiredness.

Greg H. and his wife slept in twin beds and were careful never to touch each other or demonstrate any affection. Over a period of time he had developed an inability to have intercourse. His wife felt sorry for him and "tried to make it as easy on him as possible by not bothering him about it."

Ralph B. desired his wife, but in the middle of their lovemaking his desire "short-circuited," as he described it.

Don Y.'s wife was highly demanding of her husband, often commenting on his failure to satisfy her. He soon found himself concentrating on his performance rather than on his pleasure. Finally he could not perform at all.

Harry M. had been an alcoholic for some years. After experiencing several failures to obtain an erection, he became more and more fearful.

Joe S. and his wife had always had a satisfying sexual relationship, but they both noticed a disturbing change in his ability to maintain an erection. They discussed it and then made an appointment to see his family physician.

Roger A. was in a state of depression and had no interest in sex at all. His wife could not tell the doctor whether the depression or his indifference to sex had come first.

All these men suffer from the disturbing condition known as impotence. Impotence is the inability of the husband to achieve or keep an erection sufficient for intercourse. In physical terms, the erect penis contains four or five times the volume of blood it has when flaccid. When the man experiences impotence (for whatever reason) the vascular reflex mechanism fails to pump in sufficient blood and hold the blood there to make the penis firm and keep it erect. At times the man may feel aroused and desire to make love, but his penis does not become erect. Another man suffering from impotence may be in the process of making love to his wife when his erection disappears and he reacts with panic.

Some of the most discouraged men I see in my office are those who come because of impotence. Yet these men have reason to hope, because most of those who take constructive steps toward facing and resolving their problem will regain their sexual powers. Their marriages may be even better ones afterward, for solving of the impotence problem requires the kind of loving cooperation from the wife which can greatly strengthen a couple's mutual understanding and enrich their expression of love.

While a very small percentage of men have never been able to experience an erection or ejaculation, the great majority of men seeking treatment for impotence have functioned at least fairly well until they developed a difficulty. Impotence appears in all ages, all races, on every social level, and within every economic group. At the risk of oversimplification, I will observe that impotence *usually* is caused by a man's thoughts. Seldom does a man with a positive mental attitude toward sex suffer from the condition, although *every* man at some time or other loses an erection. Therapist Helen Kaplan asserts that approximately one-half of the male population have experienced occasional times when they lost their erection or could not even get one for intercourse.

In many cases of impotence, this rather common experience of erection loss sets up a vicious cycle of failure/anxiety/more failure/more anxiety until impotence becomes the conditioned response instead of a pleasurable sex experience. Anxiety narrows into panic as the condition continues; and the keener the fear and psychic pain, the more the sufferer tries to escape by "turning off" to his wife, virtually trying to expunge sex from his life.

I particularly appreciate the opportunity to give this information on impotence to both husbands and wives who may be facing this problem. I intend now to talk to those who are involved, in the privacy of their own marriage, through the pages of this book. For others who have never experienced this condition, I suggest that they read carefully and be forewarned. Wise responses to a passing difficulty may save what could be years of grief if the temporary experience were allowed to become an established condition. The point is that in most cases it does not have to happen. An occasional experience of impotence may have no significance unless the man or his wife views it as a serious problem. Of course, impotency which changes their sex life must be dealt with.

Why is this condition so extremely devastating to the man? Because it cuts away his self-esteem where he is most vulnerable. Historically, sexual ability has been viewed as the mark of the real man— the he-man. Impotence involves the organ of his body which most represents his manhood and threatens his ego with the thought that he can no longer satisfy the woman he loves. Culturally, men have been depicted as *always* ready for sex, continually on the verge of exploding with desire, as it were. This is something an ordinary man may feel he has to try to live up to, suspecting that his own intensity of ardor falls a bit below the standard. Add to this the increasing pressure upon the husband to perform in this day when many women are preoccupied with their own needs and loudly demanding all they think they have missed. Then the slick manuals on elaborate (and often uncomfortable) new approaches to sensation and all the magazine articles on the subject being published today virtually bring the world into a man's bedroom to check on his performance. All in all, a man may feel inadequate at best, and when the worst happens— impotence—the results are both frustrating and humiliating.

The greatest mistake a man can make when troubling impotence appears is to "try not to think about it." Some men who are free to verbalize their fears with a loving, understanding wife will overcome the difficulty without even considering the need for professional help.

If the condition persists, the man should see his physician and tell him specifically what the trouble is, for he will not guess. When the doctor knows what the patient is there for, he will give him a more careful physical examination. A complete urological and endocrinological study may be required. Organic causes for impotence do exist in from five percent to ten percent of the cases, so the physician will want to rule them out at the beginning. For instance, undiagnosed diabetes or a hormonal imbalance could be at fault.

Diabetes must be given special consideration in talking about impotence. Masters and Johnson have found that forty to sixty percent of diabetics are impotent, regardless of medication or age. The impotent diabetic usually has a gradual onset of impotence over a six-to-twelve month period. Because of the selective destruction of nerve pathways almost all of these men are able to ejaculate normally, although they may be unable to have an erection at all. This means that careful understanding and consideration by the wife is essential, as this is one of the few persistent conditions which will always require that both husband and wife use manual stimulation on each other for sexual release. (Note: About 35 percent of diabetic women are also unable to reach a sexual climax by any method. This means these particular diabetic wives must learn that they can participate normally and actively in sexual intercourse and can enjoy the warmth and satisfaction of fully satisfying their husbands, but the wife will simply not be able to reach a sexual climax.)

There are a few impotent men over fifty who will benefit from testosterone (male hormone) injections. If there is benefit, it will be seen after taking a trial dosage of 100 mg of Depo-Testosterone Cypionate each week for about six weeks. The man should not take more than 600 mg in any one year, as higher dosage slightly increases the risk of developing cancer of the prostate gland. After this series of injections, the prostate should be carefully examined by digital palpatation regularly for about six months. If the six-week series of injections is helpful, a lower dosage at monthly intervals may be useful. However, there are many doctors who do not feel that testosterone is of much benefit in treating impotence except for the psychological advantage gained by the taking of the shots.

Physical causes for impotence can be readily detected, and at least 90 percent of the sufferers will be reassured to know that there is no physical impairment, that the problem is primarily a psychological one. Here are other factors the doctor will consider:

Fatigue. Simple fatigue is the most common cause of decreased sex drive in the normal man. Episodes of failing to achieve erection because of fatigue may trigger the condition of impotence. Many men come home from work with so much emotional or physical fatigue they simply do not have enough energy available for a good sexual relationship, and their failure to obtain or maintain an erection may set up the chain reaction of fear which leads to an impotent condition. A relaxed attitude of waiting till one is rested and an acceptance of lessened sexual energy when one is middle-aged will avoid much of the difficulty. Wives can help by initiating arrangements to retire at an early hour and by discouraging activities which keep their husbands from getting rest. Wives should also avoid demanding "nights out" when energy is used up in a frantic searching for entertainment and relaxation outside the home. The hours could be much better spent with just the husband and wife enjoying each other at home.

Obesity. Obesity in either husband, wife, or both may also drain away much of the strength and desire for intercourse. Obesity should be recognized as one of the most common hindrances to full arousal in the sex relationship. Obesity affects not only the physical union and contact of body parts but can also greatly interfere with the imagination factor in lovemaking, as well as lowering the individual's self-image and confidence.

Alcohol. The intake of alcohol does provoke some sexual desire, but it takes away much of the ability to perform or enjoy sexual union. Because alcohol acts as a depressant on the neurological system, it can inhibit a person's sexual functioning as much as it does his coordination or speech. The person who is an alcoholic (defined as one who has lost control of his drinking) almost never has normal sexual ability. Ninety percent of the alcoholics who have developed cirrhosis of the liver are impotent.

Drugs. Impotence in a man previously active sexually can be caused by the taking of certain medications. Here are some of the common drugs which have been found to contribute to impotence or decreased sexual drive in a man:

Amphetamines
Atropine
Banthine
Barbiturates
Cortisone
Estrogen
Guanethidine (Esimil)
Imipramine (Tofranil, Presamine, Janimine, Imavate, SK-Pramine)
Methyldopa (Aldomet)

Monoamine Oxidase Inhibitors (Parnate, Marplan, Nardil)
Narcotics
Progesterone
Propantheline Bromide (Pro-Banthine)
Psychotropic Agents, including Tricyclics
Reserpine
Sedatives of all types
Tranquilizers

Note that the illegal narcotics and stimulants of today's drug culture are offenders. One would like to tell young couples that as they seek thrills in one area of life they may be robbing themselves of some of the really great thrills available in a positive, growing relationship in sex in marriage.

Depression. It is important for the doctor to determine whether the depression has brought on the impotence, or whether the condition of impotence has brought on the depression. A person who is clinically depressed has a low appetite for food, sleep, pleasures, sex, and for life itself. Most of this person's energy is directed toward survival in the face of continuing despair, and it is understandable when there is no appetite for things normally enjoyed. Appropriate counseling and medication are indicated and usually produce positive results.

Sometimes a man will suffer depression because of something which has happened in his life. It could be the death of a friend or the loss of a job, or any other disturbing happening. The depression may well trigger sexual inability, but this should be only a temporary situation. Sexual desire is sometimes absent for months after such serious illnesses as a heart attack or a stroke, because of the depression brought on by the illness.

Other Negative Feelings. Any negative feelings such as anger or jealousy which break a man's concentration in lovemaking and drain off sexual energy can bring on impotence. Putting biblical principles into action will avoid much of this. If clashes in the marriage are handled in a constructive manner when they arise, unspoken hostility will not carry over into the sexual relationship. If a couple feel free to make love when they go to bed, this is a good indication that concealed anger has been dealt with.

Dismay Over Decreased Vigor. The man over fifty must accept normal changes in his sexual capabilities. If he tries to hold himself to his twenty-one-year-old performance, he will at times fail and may experience acute anxiety. If he adapts gracefully to minor physiological changes, he can enjoy sex for many years to come. He should remember that what he has "lost" in youthful vigor he has gained in capacity to express his love in a mature, more meaningful, and more skillful manner.

Any Unusual Stress. Any stress in a man's life can express itself through impotency. After all, the very word *impotence* suggests weakness, feebleness, helplessness, inability, and lack of power, strength, vigor, and capacity. When these feelings attack because of stress, it is perhaps natural that they find the sexual function a vulnerable target. It will be helpful to remember that one cannot *will* an erection. A tense man trying to force an erection of his penis will be unable to do so. Relaxation and concentration on pleasurable sensations without any feeling of forcing one's body to perform will be the best and the only approach at such times.

Seeing Sex as Sin. Sometimes in a man's early upbringing he has encountered the erroneous belief that sex is sin, and later in life, after he is married, this may lead to unexpressed guilt, even fear of touching his wife. His normal sexual reaction, then, is short-circuited, and his conscious-mind censor refuses to let erection happen; instead, it represses the trigger mechanism. When he is asleep, of course, he will have nocturnal emissions, and sometimes in the morning, like most healthy men, he will have erections. His impotence is psychogenic, but it can be resolved with professional help and a right understanding of God's Word.

Poor Learning Experiences. Sometimes early in marriage men who fumble and struggle in trying to insert the penis, and in the process lose their erection, set up a sensitivity which may produce impotence. The male feels foolish; his self-esteem is damaged. And besides that, he loses his concentration on sensation when he has to stop to try to find the place for the penis to go. This is why the wife should always assist in inserting the penis even when there is no problem with impotence. She is the one who knows best where it belongs.

The Primary Problem

Beyond all other factors in impotence is the primary problem: The husband is too intensely preoccupied with his ability or inability to achieve and maintain an erection. He is pressured by the fear of failure. He concentrates on his bodily reactions like a spectator at his own lovemaking until self-consciousness destroys all joy and abandonment and sensation of pleasure. He tries, without success, to command the sexual reflexes, but they respond only to desire and stimulation. He becomes like the person who "can't do anything right." "I'm all thumbs today," such a person complains, and from then on pays attention to his failures, not his successes. So the anxious lover fumbles and concentrates on his fumbles until he is aware of nothing else. Self-consciousness is always self-defeating. It always produces an unsatisfactory state of affairs; never more so than in the lovemaking process. It opens the door to fear of failure, the true villain behind the scenes, and any cure must deal with this fear.

What has happened to the wife during the development of impotency? She is apt to be in one of three camps: (1) Feeling rejected and taking the blame; (2) Feeling rejected and reacting with hostility; or (3) Trying to understand and wanting to help in the most mature and loving way possible—if only someone will tell her how.

I cannot emphasize enough to the wife that she very well may be the one who holds the key to the cure for her husband. The cooperation of a loving partner in restoring a man to sexual vigor cannot be overestimated. When I see such a wife ready to work with her husband—loyal and caring, more concerned about him than about her own ego—I have great confidence that the husband will be cured.

To the wife in the first camp: A woman who has difficulty in accepting herself may view the husband's impotency as a personal rejection of her, when in reality it is another problem altogether. She may take it as proof of her own inadequacy as a woman, when instead it may in no way reflect her husband's disinterest. In fact, men are most apt to fear failure with the woman they love, while they could perform effectively with a woman they are indifferent to. Someone has pointed out that *love* and *erection* are not synonymous words. Her frustrated husband may have a great deal of desire but no accompanying erection. So to such a woman, I suggest that she choose to think rationally about herself, her husband, and the situation. When she refuses to put herself down and instead puts herself at her husband's disposal as they work together for a cure, she will take significant steps toward the kind of emotional maturity which will make her far more desirable than ever before.

I have noted that some of the women who complain most about their husbands' not being able to satisfy them sexually turn out to be the least cooperative when it comes to working together to solve the problem. To the hostile wife, I should point out that she is only defeating herself, for she and the husband she is undermining are still one flesh in the eyes of God. In helping her husband she will do a great service to herself and will perhaps find the love she inwardly longs for as she learns to give.

To that woman who is mature, stable, sensitive, and acceptant of her husband's needs, I say that she can work wonders—and she will! In the process, even without intercourse, there can be a good deal of mutual pleasure as well.

The two begin by admitting that they have a problem—a *couple* problem—which can be solved. As they move toward a solution, they will be ridding one another of the buildup of feelings of inadequacy. What a gift to give!

The solution involves three lines of approach, which we might call in easy-to-remember terms *talk, touch,* and *teasing*.

Talk refers to establishment of broken communication lines, lines that have been battered down by periods of indifference and frustration. The wife must help her husband to put his fears into words. The conspiracy of silence is now broken, and the man must be able to express how he feels. As each is open to the feelings of the other, a climate of understanding and tender togetherness grows.

Touch refers to physical communication, which may also have broken down as each moved to his own side of the bed after periods of frustration. The husband and the wife must begin again to enjoy the fun and pleasure of affection, of cuddling and caressing and sleeping close together.

Teasing suggests the kind of sexual relationship which can begin to develop even though the husband is still unable (or thinks he is unable) to gain an erection. The couple should agree to spend time together pleasuring each other without any demand for intercourse. The husband should use the new communication lines to tell his wife exactly what gives him pleasure. Her body is available to him, and his body is available to her. Let them enjoy caressing each other in love play without expecting anything further. The wife should demand nothing of him in terms of arousal; some therapists suggest that the couple agree to prohibit intercourse and orgasm for several days. They should simply relax together in a warm, intimate situation while he learns to let his body take over with the proper responses. In this setting of leisurely erotic stimulation without sexual intercourse, the penis erection will wax and wane. The husband will discover that once an erection is obtained, it will come back if it goes away. To observe it come and go is an important part of the training process for both husband and wife, as they gain experiential knowledge that with loving cooperation the erection will always return.

When the time seems right the husband will find delight in satisfying his wife by stimulation of the clitoris. When he feels ready for intercourse, the wife should be prepared to insert the penis. Even if it is only partially erect, she can "stuff" the penis in the vagina, and the subsequent stimulation will often increase and maintain the erection.

It has been found that the male-above position is usually the most satisfying and stimulating position for men experiencing difficulty with erection.

The lovemaking process should never be rushed. There is enough time to regain full sexual powers, and the love play should be carried out in a most pleasurable, leisurely, and sensual manner. Privacy should be ensured. The wife should wear her most appealing gown (which may be no gown at all), and the husband should use the endearing names he once called her. Nicknames can be very unstimulating. (Ever hear a man call his wife *Mom*? Too often if he calls her this he will subconsciously visualize her as mother, thus losing sexual interest.)

Once gentle stimulation and erotic encounters have turned the tide, remember that success breeds more success. The husband should realize, however, that fears of failure in sexual performance could come back at any time, perhaps when he is in a stress-filled situation. He can find a cure the way he found the first one—by turning to his wife, sharing his fears, finding comfort and pleasure in her body, relaxing and refusing to *demand* any performance from himself.

The wife must be careful not to make him feel inferior, never to put him under pressure, never to judge his sexual performance. She must be responsive and seductive, yet not come on too strong in her actions. Together they can make the most of their sexual relationship—perhaps finding far more pleasure in each other than they ever did before the difficulty developed.

A rate of cure of impotence of 50 to 75 percent is reported by secular therapists. I have no exact statistics to quote, but I have observed a rate of cure which is much higher for the Christian husband who claims and uses his extra resource against the main villain—*fear* of failure. God has given us resources far greater than the spirit of fear, and resting in that knowledge will provide the Christian husband with a stability and relaxation that can go far in solving almost every impotency problem. The Bible says, "For God hath not given us the spirit of fear, but of power, and of love, and of a sound mind" (2 Timothy 1:7).

Every situation of life in which we see our own inadequacy can be an opportunity to see the power of Christ undertake for us. No need is too small or too great for our God to meet, we discover as we count on Him!

9

The "Perfect" Wife

by Gaye Wheat

This will not be one of those very serious lectures on how to become the *perfect* wife! I don't want to imply that I have somehow attained that state, or that it is possible for you to get there by following ten easy steps and putting forth a little effort.

The chapter title with *perfect* in quotation marks should suggest that we will be using *perfect* in a somewhat different manner from that which the dictionary decrees with its list of lofty definitions:

"Without blemish or defect" (*Who, me?*)
"Completely skilled" (*Hardly!*)
"Thoroughly effective" (*Maybe occasionally.*)
"Having all the qualities necessary . . ." (*Well, no.*)

But then that last definition gives pause for thought: *Having all the qualities necessary* . . . to assure your husband that you're the perfect wife for him. There it is! Exactly what this chapter is about.

We know we aren't perfect wives. And our husbands know it too. But it is possible to keep them so happy that they think of us as perfect, because in the details which matter most to them, we have learned to please them! Now, I am not talking about devious dealings or cute manipulations designed to befuddle our husbands into adoring us. They are not that easily fooled. And, most importantly, there is a better way to please them—a way that God can honor because it is rooted in the New Testament principle of servanthood: "Ourselves your servants for Jesus' sake" (2 Corinthians 4:5).

Of course this does not mean that we are to behave like menials around our husbands. To serve one's husband for Jesus' sake does not demand that one be servile and abject like a Babylonian slave or an eighteenth-century washerwoman. *It begins with the attitude of thinking about him instead of being preoccupied with myself.* It includes looking for ways, all the time, to help him and please him. In the words of Proverbs 31, this kind of wife will do her husband "good and not evil, all the days of her life." The behavior that pleases him flows out of an inner attitude that I have already chosen for myself—the attitude that my husband is the king of my household and the king of my marriage. Next to the Lord he is the one I want to please the most. He is my top priority, right after Christ. So it is my joy and privilege to treat my husband as my "lord." And here I am in good company, for Peter in his first epistle instructs the Christian wives to adapt themselves to their husbands, their beauty "the unfading loveliness of a calm and gentle spirit, a thing very precious in the eyes of God" (1 Peter 3:4 PHILLIPS), and he goes on to point to Sarah as a good example: "Even as Sarah obeyed Abraham, calling him lord . . . (1 Peter 3:6).

The rewards of this attitude have been mentioned earlier, but they are worth repeating: The more you please your husband, the more he is going to be eager to please you. The more he attempts to please you, the more you are going to be happy and satisfied, so even more you are going to try to do the things which make him happy. This is the glorious cycle of response which we could call a circle, for a circle never ends. Once we step into that circle of love, we will not want to move out, and although our husbands may still know our limitations only too well, they will feel that whatever we do is *all right*. We have proved ourselves to be just the right wives for them.

When it comes to the sex relationship, we *must* be pleased ourselves in order to please our husbands. Men who rate their sexual experience as outstanding say that they get so much out of it because of the pleasure they receive from seeing their wives excited and thrilled. Most husbands realize there is far more to sex in marriage than having their biological needs met by a passive, tired, or bored, but submissive wife. They want to see their wives sent into ecstasies by their lovemaking; and yet, according to statistics, less than 40 percent of married couples consistently enjoy maximum fulfillment and release in intercourse.

Because I speak at seminars on sexual technique in marriage, women often talk to me about their disappointments and their longings in this area. They know they don't have a good sex relationship, but they suspect everyone else does. And they are *not* happy.

On the basis of our counseling experience, as well as the evidence of the Scriptures, Dr. Wheat and I believe that good sex is a must for a good marriage. It may not be the most important thing, but if either partner is deprived of sex or dissatisfied with it, then it becomes a major issue. A *satisfactory* sex relationship strengthens any marriage. In fact, a oneness in this intimate area often indicates that every part of the marriage will be reinforced.

Even though sex is such a public topic these days, women still come to me who have been married for thirty years and do not know whether or not they have ever reached a climax. All the general discussion of sex in the magazines has not helped them. They need to understand the specifics of the sex experience, with its arousal, response, and release, and that is why we have made this book so very specific.

The factual, physiological information in *Intended for Pleasure*, correctly put into action, will take care of less than half the problem for dissatisfied women and their husbands. What is left unsolved falls into the categories of attitude and communication. Some counselors have suggested that as much as 80 percent of the difficulty lies in these areas.

Evaluation. I have this suggestion for those of you who are longing for a better sex life or for you who admit (without longing) that it isn't all that great for your husband. Take stock of your own attitudes first! This calls for some time alone when you can honestly evaluate your attitudes toward sex and toward your husband as a lover. Before you are done, you will find that you are taking a long look at your self-esteem as well, for that too occupies a place in the total picture.

Begin with your attitude toward sex in general. When you read the word *sex*, what do you think about? What image comes into your mind? Something warm and loving and tender and yielding? Or perhaps something a bit distasteful, or even unpleasant?

What was your attitude before you were married? Did your mother tell you everything you needed to know beforehand? Did she tell you *any-*

thing? Perhaps you thought your husband would know it all, and yet he didn't. Do you still have sexual inhibitions? Do you endure sex as a duty, or anticipate it with delight? Are you warm and responsive to your husband's lovemaking, or do you scoot over to the other side of the bed, hoping he won't show any interest?

Did your honeymoon experiences disappoint you or turn you off, establishing an unhappy pattern which has not yet been broken? I cannot count how many women have told me their first experiences in marriage were very disappointing: "The moon did not glow . . . the stars did not fall . . . and no lightning . . . flashed at all!" Can you accept this disappointment, which perhaps still programs your reactions, by understanding that the difficulties you and your husband experienced were probably due to a lack of information and hopes too high for the moment you had been waiting for? Although romantic literature has implied that as soon as you are man and wife all your sexual responses are automatically released, this is just not true. The sex act is not instinctive. It takes time to establish a truly great sex relationship.

Here's a way of evaluating your contribution to the physical love relationship, suggested by Shirley Rice in *Physical Unity in Marriage*. She says that we women should try measuring our *physical* love for our husbands by the yardstick in 1 Corinthians 13, the great love chapter. See how you do. Remember we're talking now about *physical* love. Is yours patient and kind? Never envious or jealous? Not possessive? Not conceited? Never rude? Never indiscreet? Not insistent upon its own right? Not self-seeking? Never touchy, fretful, or resentful? Does it pay no attention to a suffered wrong? Not count up past wrongs? Rejoice not at wrongdoing, but at the truth? Does it always believe the best of him? Does it ever fail?

What a strict measuring stick! We are just not capable of that quality of love without God's power. But the point is that we can have the enabling of God's power as women born again in Christ to remake and transform every wrong attitude we have found in ourselves during this evaluation time.

Let's continue the evaluation by considering just how we look at *ourselves*. Do you accept yourself the way you are? Or do you feel inwardly that you are unattractive? Either overweight or underweight? You think perhaps your hips are too big or your legs too skinny? Or you don't have enough bust? (And you know how men seem to look at full busts.)

When you and your husband make love, are you anxious to keep covered with a long gown, or to turn out all the lights, so that he won't see your deficiencies or blemishes? And doesn't this affect your behavior during the process? You aren't quite free; you never quite forget yourself and how you look!

Most of us know that we do not have figures to compare to Raquel Welch's or the legendary Marilyn Monroe's. So it is hard for us to accept the fact that our husbands might think that we with our ho-hum bodies are beautiful or desirable. I believe this is a bigger issue with most women than they will ever let on. The problem is compounded if you have the kind of husband who never says anything encouraging or complimentary to you. A woman who feels beautiful is going to be beautiful for her husband when they are alone together—and much more uninhibited in lovemaking. You and I should remember that our husbands chose us, not Raquel, and that if they get the loving response they want, they'll never think about our imperfections.

While we are evaluating, it is time for every woman to ask herself if she accepts her husband just as he is. Not only in appearance, but with the kind of temperament, strengths and weaknesses, and even the earning ability that he possesses. You see, this has a definite effect upon the way you respond to him in lovemaking, or the way he approaches you. If you cut him down in word or thought, your relationship will be damaged. After acceptance of your mate just as he is, it is time to concentrate on his strengths and focus your thoughts on them. How about a few compliments for him? As women, we may expect to be always on the receiving end. How about telling him how glad you are that he knows how to repair your car or your washing machine himself? Or how much you appreciate his kindness to your parents? Or how you admire his good taste in clothes? Or how wonderful it is to have such a physically strong husband, or a husband who gives you such wise advice when you need it? Or whatever applies to your own man. It is all a matter of honest appreciation, which you pass on to him instead of keeping it to yourself. The couple who appreciate each other and *show it* have every reason to expect a wonderful sexual relationship. Difficulties in their situation are more apt to be only physical in nature, matters of adjustment which can be readily solved by applying proper information.

Communication. After evaluating attitudes, you need to consider your communication. Sex without communication has little to commend it. Your communication may be of the nonverbal kind during the lovemaking process itself. Perhaps you have learned to do what the sex therapists suggest—to put your hand lovingly over your husband's and show him where you want stimulation. Or, if he is too rough or too gentle, to show him again with your hand over his. There are ways of telling him when you are ready for intercourse without saying a word. But even before you make love, you may need to communicate your needs to your husband frankly and clearly. He may have needs to tell you about, too. If you want to reach orgasm and are not doing so, ask him to give you the manual stimulation that will afford you release. It is amazing how silent we women are on something as important as the sex act in marriage. We *wish* in silence or we *suffer* in silence or we *hope* that this time he will be different, that this time he will think of doing that which we long for him to do. Why not just tell him?

While we are speaking of communication, let me caution you about one thing which is better left uncommunicated. Some wives out of a desire to please their husbands (or for other reasons) have pretended for years that they are wildly enjoying his lovemaking, when really they never even reach a release. Now with all the talk in magazine articles about attaining orgasm, they realize that they could have it after all—if only their husband knew what to do. But the poor man thinks he has been doing it all these years. Some women in an attempt at honesty tell their husbands they have been faking a response. The results of this can be almost disastrous. We have known husbands whose egos were crushed by this revelation. When they found out that their wives had been pretending all along, they were so disgusted they would have nothing further to do with them. Realizing that the wife has been living a lie, a husband may well wonder what other areas of the relationship have been dishonest as well. I believe that the husband, in most cases, is better off not knowing. If you have painted yourself into a corner by pretense, you'll have to work yourself out of it with wisdom and a lot of prayer. Make some graceful suggestions to your husband concerning techniques you've read about, without implying that he has failed to arouse or satisfy you all this time. As these techniques are tried, you may find pretense becoming a wonderful reality.

Attitudes and Action.   After evaluation time is over, action should begin. You may feel, as some women have expressed to me, that even though you know your attitudes are not right, you just *can't* change them. The person who says he can't, *can't*. He is already committed to failure.

On the other hand, the woman who has the enabling power of God within her *can* change. How does it happen? By turning your attitude over to the Lord and then beginning to be and say and do what you know is right. Realize that as you please your husband, you *are* both obeying and pleasing the Lord. Let it be a love-offering to both. The Lord will not *make* you do anything; He will not change you without your cooperation. You are not a robot or a puppet on a string. But if you know the attitude you should have, then you have to say, "Okay, with God's strength operating in me, I am going to be different." And then begin to *do it*. How does a woman quit biting her nails? Not by saying *I can't*, but by quitting. The principle is the same in changing your attitudes toward love, sex, marriage, and your husband.

There are a number of things you might consider to make sex more enjoyable for both of you. First, let me suggest the "tool" of anticipation—particularly if you have had some faulty attitudes concerning the sex experience. A period of romantic anticipation for sex, building up all day and ending happily in bed, can very much enhance the love relationship. Your husband has the opportunity to stir your interest and increase his own anticipation. For instance, if he gives you a very meaningful kiss when he leaves for work and then phones you sometime during the day just because he's thinking of you and missing you, the stage is being set for a responsive welcome to his lovemaking after the children have been put to bed. If your husband does not yet know that response is greatly influenced by preliminary courtship, perhaps that is one of the things you will need to communicate to him. Along with mental anticipation, make some definite plans to take care of meals, children, and responsibilities so that you will have uninterrupted time to spend with your husband at the end of the day.

The best way to change your attitude about sex is to start thinking and acting positively, for better feelings always follow correct action. If your problem is that it takes you so *long* to get aroused, then start anticipating early in the day. Begin concentrating on the thought that sex with your husband is pleasant. Later when lovemaking occurs, keep thinking: *This is pleasing to my body. This is pleasing to me. This is what God created for me. I want to please my husband; this is going to be a happy experience. I am going to feel sensations that are pleasant and wonderful. . . .*

This will greatly help you unless your husband just does not provide any wonderful sensations. In that case, offer him this book to read, so that he can learn how to pleasure his wife!

If you want to be able to enjoy sex for what you receive from it as well as for what it does for your husband, you are going to have to take the responsibility for your own sexual pleasure and not hesitate to communicate your needs to your husband. You are going to have to be very open with him if you hope to develop the abandonment which will give you the most pleasurable sex. Both of you need to establish that rejection of a particular form of love play is not rejection of the *person*, only the *action*. Each of you must be willing to give and to receive suggestions in order to increase excitement. We women do not hesitate to communicate our need for a new dress or a new carpet, but when it comes to our sexual needs, we seem to clam up. Do not ever think a problem is too small or insignificant to be discussed.

While in the process of lovemaking, concentration is most important. Even though you may have been building anticipation and practicing new attitudes, you will find that you can be easily distracted and then have to start all over again in seeking arousal. You cannot allow yourself to lie there thinking about the problems of the day or about the fact that you forgot to take the meat out of the freezer. You need to keep your mind and body working together. Concentrate on whatever will arouse your desire. Think of the joy you are experiencing as you and your husband possess one another.

Be active, not passive, and you will enjoy lovemaking more. If you are active, your attention is less likely to wander. Do not be afraid to caress your husband while he is caressing you. When you abandon yourself to pursuing release, you will become more aware of your sensations, and your body will automatically begin to move about to help increase stimulation.

By the way, have you ever initiated sex? Almost every husband finds this an exciting development. The occasional husband who feels threatened by it is often one who fears his own sexual inadequacy. Tim Timmons in his Maximum Marriage Seminars says, "Sweep him off his feet . . . go get him . . . *go after him.*" Without saying one word, you can let your husband know that you think he is wonderful and that you find him physically attractive and desirable.

Perhaps there has been a difference of opinion on what frequency of intercourse is desirable. Whatever the two of you together prefer certainly is "normal" for your marriage. If you think your husband seems to require sex a lot more than you do, ponder this illustration: If you were in the desert and you were thirsty, you'd think about a glass of water, wouldn't you? But if you're standing by the refrigerator, and there's a big pitcher of ice-cold water inside the door, and you know you can open the door and get it any time you want to, the need for a drink is not nearly so urgent. Maybe the reason your husband seems never to think of anything besides sex is that he's "in the desert" and "thirsty."

Sometimes you will be very tired and feeling as sexy as an old sock, but your husband will approach you with desire. Secular therapists say a wife should be able to respond, "Sorry, but I'm just not up to it tonight." My own opinion as a Christian wife is that we can depend on the Lord to give us the strength and ability to be as warm and responsive as our husbands desire, no matter how tired we are. As we commit this in prayer, trusting the Lord to give us the strength to meet our husbands' needs, we often find not only that we can do it, but that we enjoy the experience as well. The heart of the matter is attitude. Please do not be like the lady who told me grimly, "I have never *refused* him." And yet it was obvious that the refusal was there in her heart and even in her voice.

If you find rebellion rising within because of counsel which seems to stress submission to your husband and thus goes against your natural inclination, remember that submission to our God and to our husbands is a supernatural work, the result of our own choice of action *plus* God's power. Psalms 40:8 says, "I delight to do thy will, O my God," and this is the point a wife must reach. Submission is always done *by* you, and not *to* you.

Ritual can become a hindrance to sexual enjoyment. If you and your husband have been having sex always at the same time and in exactly the same routine, try a different time and a different approach. As the wife who usually schedules the activities for the family, you can plan times when you and your husband will be rested and ready for each other. Your husband needs energy for a good sexual relationship, and you can sometimes protect him from the exhaustion which comes from adding social activities on top of his daily work load.

Your Appearance. Both of you will enjoy sex more if *you* feel that your appearance is at its best. Of course this is not always possible, especially at those times when lovemaking occurs spontaneously. But at bedtime your husband will enjoy seeing you at your bathed and prettiest feminine best. And your confidence in your own desirability will rise accordingly. A filmy nightgown creates an aura of loveliness. There are some "granny" gowns that even Granny would not wear, and your husband's old college T-shirt probably doesn't do much for a woman either. However, if that is what your husband wants you to wear, then by all means sleep in it. Some of you may be thinking that your husband couldn't care less what you wear to bed, just so you take it off at the right time. Nevertheless, a clean, perfumed body attired in a feminine gown tells him that you care enough about your time with him to be your most appealing and desirable. Now we all know that a husband is greatly stimulated by seeing his wife's body, but there can be too much of anything, even nudity. Often going about the house nude or only scantily clad is not a good practice. As a wife once told me, "A little something left to the imagination is especially enticing."

Of course appearance before your husband at any time becomes an important issue. Have you noticed on television dramas that when scriptwriters want to show a marriage is dead, they portray the wife wearing an ugly robe, with her hair up in curlers? The other clues are that she repulses her husband when he attempts to be affectionate, and she generally wears a drawn, down-at-the-mouth look and often cries or complains. We have here some clues for the wife who *wants* to please her husband: Look pretty . . . keep smiling . . . don't complain . . . receive your husband with open arms!

There are other ways to please, so simple that you know them. But we all need reminding. Give extra attention to the beauty and comfort of your bedroom. Keep the house picked up late in the afternoon so that there will be an appearance of order, even if you have not had time to clean. Freshen up yourself too before your husband comes home. Serve broccoli if that's his vegetable, and leave off the green beans which he detests. Wear the blue dress that he likes best. If he prefers to stay up late at night, try to squeeze in an afternoon nap and stay up late with him. If he enjoys baseball, learn to like it. You don't do these things because you are a doormat, but because you *want* to. Most important, a wise wife will not argue. She will keep her husband peaceful and satisfied and happy by gracefully conceding to his wishes or deferring to his opinions. When the issue is an important one, then it can be decided on its merits rather than being just another thing to wrangle about. To remind ourselves to listen more and talk less is always good advice for the wife. And all this fits with the admonitions in God's Word for wives to adapt themselves to their husbands.

If we want to be more beautiful for our husbands, we'll be careful not to let ourselves go as we get older and feel satisfied with each other. Especially, if our husbands do not want us to be fat, we will avoid adding those ten pounds a year that pull us out of shape. But more importantly, do not neglect inner beauty. Alice Painter says that when a woman is sixteen, she can't help it if she isn't beautiful. But if she is sixty and not beautiful, it's her fault! A woman who is miserable on the inside will show it in her wrinkles and her countenance. She will show it in her actions—the hasty push-away action which repulses. She will reveal it in her voice, which may be loud and strident, or whining and complaining, or ridiculing in tone. The woman who is loved and knows she is loved, who loves the Lord and loves her husband, *will* be lovely.

The Security of Christian Love. I have been asked how my marriage has changed since Ed and I became Christians some fifteen years ago. There is no comparison! Before that time, of course, we were both self-centered. We did not have the kind of sex relationship spoken of in this book because we just did not care that much about pleasing each other, and we were quite ignorant of the meaning of sex in God's Word. We got along well together, but we did not share our innermost feelings with each other.

Now that we are Christians, I know that the love Ed has for me is the same kind of love that Christ has for me. I am safe and secure in that love. I know that I can always talk to my husband and that I can trust his wisdom as the spiritual leader of our family. As we have become so used to pouring our hearts out together in prayer, we now are free to communicate about anything to each other. We are not afraid to expose ourselves and our faults, because we know that we accept each other just as we are, with all our frailties and faults and good points. How wonderful it is to know that I am not on a performance basis: No matter how poorly I perform, I am still going to be loved. And that *has* to make me perform better.

Is it a perfect relationship? Of course not! I still have attitudes rise up within me that are not right. Then I have to back up and start again, turning it over to the Lord, knowing that I don't *have* to act this way as a Christian. I don't *have* to let my old nature be in control, and I need not choose to be childish and peeved about some insignificant thing that my ego felt as a slight. Actually, when I stop and consider a moment, I know that my husband was busy or occupied and that he did not mean whatever was said or done. As a Christian woman I am free to be obedient to God and pleasing to my husband. I do not *have* to behave in any other way.

I would like to think that the husbands are reading this chapter and that they will begin to show their wives how much they love them and appreciate them—not just in the bedroom, but at any time, with hugs and pats and kind, complimentary words. *Many a man does not realize that the wife he has is a reflection of his own behavior toward her.*

Children and Priorities.   Two things should be said about the children in this discussion of sex and marriage. First, that they should be in the proper line of priorities. Our husbands must come first and the children after that. Some women get the children mixed up there ahead of the husband; then when the children are grown and gone, the husband and wife have nothing to communicate to one another. Second, our home is where our children first pick up attitudes concerning sex. The best sex education they can receive is to know that mother and dad love each other and to see this love expressed in tender, considerate ways.

Here is an example to show how a child's attitudes are influenced: Suppose that you are standing at the kitchen range preparing supper, and your husband walks by and pats you on the behind. You turn around and in a rebuking tone say, "Quit that!" And little Johnny and Susie, playing nearby, observe what has taken place. Do you see the lesson they have just learned? But now let's play the scene again. Suppose your husband walks by and pats you on the behind and you turn around and grin at him, maybe reach out, and both of you put your arms around each other and exchange a kiss. He goes over to sit down and read the newspaper, and you hum a little tune while stirring the food. What a different lesson the children have just learned!

Yes, your children will observe your actions and absorb your attitudes. If they see that you and your husband have a warm, demonstrative relationship between you, they will be more likely to grow up to be affectionate themselves and to have a healthy attitude about sex. Perhaps later on you will then have the privilege of helping to prepare them for marriage.

Advice for Brides. Some of you may be the mothers of teenage daughters who will very shortly (before you are ready) be considering marriage. Recent brides have told me that they wish someone had shared a few honeymoon suggestions with them. For this reason, I want to include the following hints: Make all your wedding preparations far enough in advance so that there are no last-minute details for which you are responsible. . . . Be rested. This means no girl-talk until the wee hours of the morning of the wedding and no bachelor party that last night. . . . Plan a *short* trip for the first night. . . . Be certain to pack a tube of K-Y Jelly. . . . Have a small towel handy to absorb the secretions. . . . Decide beforehand what you both expect on the wedding night. . . . Establish if you both want to remove all of each other's clothing or if you want to come floating into the bedroom in your gorgeous white negligee and sweep him off his feet. The barrier of seeing each other naked is best broken at some time during your first night together. . . . Take a shower together at least once on your honeymoon trip. . . . Oh, yes . . . take along a candle for atmosphere lighting. Relax and anticipate the cherishing and possessing of each other.

Ladies, I have a choice Father's Day card from Hallmark which goes to my husband every year because the message is so perfect. It says:

To my husband, who still gives me
   protection
     attention
      security
       grocery money
        and . . .
          GOOSE BUMPS!

And he does! I want you to discover that the principles in this chapter work when they are put into practice and that as you learn to please your husband and to be pleased by him, you'll have all the goose bumps you could want. It begins with you and your attitude.

10

All Love, All Liking, All Delight

A traveler from outer space, able to read current literature on sex in marriage, might easily gain the impression that married love consists of a physical sensation lasting only a few seconds which everyone is trying for; and this same visitor to our planet might well ask, in his own way, "If that's all there is to the mating process of these creatures, what's all the fuss about?"

Of course there is much, much more—"all love, all liking, all delight," in the words of Robert Herrick. But the secular world has become preoccupied with physical technique; much of the Christian world is debating the implications of the biblical order of relationships in Ephesians 5; and seldom does anyone venture into the area between, where the dynamics of the sexual union in marriage are considered—not physical techniques, not the deep underlying principles, but *how* two people committed in marriage actually interact in love to approach the "one flesh" experience.

After the Bible has dealt with the basic order of husband and wife (sacrificial love and submission), it leaves much to our own understanding concerning these dynamics of the sexual relationship. The Bible's silence does not imply that the last word has already been said, but rather that God in His vast good sense allows each of His creatures to explore the unlimited possibilities inherent in the relationship He Himself thought up. These unlimited possibilities somehow converge into an offering which two people make of themselves to each other, an offering which reflects all that they are separately and all that they will become together.

Without trying to pin down the specifics, which will be as different in every marriage as the individuals involved, we can make these observations about the dynamics of the sexual relationship between man and wife:

First, the sexual relationship is meant to be full of life, rich in emotion, and ever-changing within the security of the marriage commitment. When lovemaking takes on a tiresome sameness of routine, both partners may feel a vague sense of dissatisfaction with unnamed longings, even though they do not realize that something precious is missing. That missing something, of course, is the free and active expression of a living love! In such cases, their love needs to be renewed or liberated.

Sometimes a dull routine develops because either husband or wife fears change and tries to keep the act of love static as a security measure. That individual is unwittingly choosing emptiness, not fullness. The choice becomes another form of burying one's goods in the ground, because one is "afraid." The Lord Jesus was not pleased with that approach; nor do we think He is pleased with a lifeless, emotionally barren relationship.

What keeps the relationship vital and moving is a joyous pattern of mutual response, the kind we see pictured in the ever-changing relationship of Solomon and his bride in Song of Solomon. The two lovers had periods of almost indescribable pleasure interspersed with changes of fortune and diversities of feeling. Theirs was not a perfect relationship, because they were human. When he wanted her, at one point, she did not wish to be disturbed. Then after he had turned away, her heart was moved for him, and she sought him until they were reunited. Their reunion became a glorious blending of mutual pleasure as he poured forth words of intense appreciation—"How fair and how pleasant art thou, O love, for delights. . ."—and she passionately assured him that her delights were all for him.

Those almost perfect moments that sometimes happen between lovers tempt us to become collectors, trying to capture and repeat our favorite experiences. They are pleasant to remember, but a clinging to the past often causes us to miss out on the new delights which are still ahead. The time when our love relationship is admittedly less than perfect will always leave room for movement toward each other. As long as we are committed to each other, we need not fear the constant change within marriage, the ebb and flow of the relationship of two lovers, for it is a sign of life.

C. S. Lewis somehow caught the essence of that continuing change in a few vivid phrases describing his own marriage: "H. and I feasted on love; every mode of it—solemn and merry, romantic and realistic, sometimes as dramatic as a thunderstorm, sometimes as comfortable and unemphatic as putting on your soft slippers. No cranny of heart or body remained unsatisfied" (from *A Grief Observed*).

If the relationship is constantly changing, so are the needs of the two people involved. Therefore, our second observation is that there is no fixed part for each mate to play within the sexual experience. For instance, there can be no "boss" in the mutuality of coming together. While the man is to be tenderly protective, there is no place in love for a rigid dominance on his part. To say that a wife is to be submissive in the overall pattern of the home does not imply that in the sexual relationship she is limited to awaiting his pleasure. She has the equal privilege of initiating the act of love and of offering her own imaginative style of pleasure to the total relationship.

Each can be most truly himself or herself in this particular area of the marriage, with neither locked into a role which must be played again and again. The husband may be essentially a strong personality, but there are times in the privacy of their love when he will want to be dependent upon his wife and free to express this. She may sometimes need the knowledge of his strength, and should be free both to be that which he needs and to seek that which she needs. Together each can give the emotional sustenance which the other requires. In such a relationship fantasized sex will be discarded as something outgrown, as much less than the real thing.

Surely part of the delight of the relationship is that opportunity in the privacy of your bedroom to be all that you know you can be, yet may never show the rest of the world. "God be thanked," said Robert Browning. "The meanest of his creatures boasts two soul-sides, one to face the world with, one to show a woman when he loves her!" You can be most totally your true self with your mate.

Perhaps others think of you as stiff, cool, reserved. But here with your partner you laugh together; you are free to be passionate or tender as the mood strikes you, protective or dependent, flirtatious or surrendered.

There should be room in the sexual relationship for all parts of your personality to be expressed at one time or another. And all the while the expression of your own being meets the need of your mate. "How do I love thee?" wrote Elizabeth Barrett Browning in *Sonnets from the Portuguese*, in one of the world's most famous love poems. "I love thee to the level of everyday's most quiet need, by sun and candlelight."

Our third observation concerns the importance of a lighthearted approach to lovemaking in marriage. Sex with your partner is far more than recreation, of course, but it is that as well: the best, the most relaxing, renewing recreation known to man, and God planned that too. No wonder it is often called "love *play*." It is fun, not duty; high excitement, not boredom; something to anticipate, not a dreary experience to be avoided if you can. It should be and it can be the highlight of any ordinary day, as two people come together to refresh themselves in each other's love, to find forgetfulness from the cares and insults of life, and to experience the total and wonderful relaxation God designed as the culmination of the lovemaking, with both husband and wife reaching release. How ironic that couples search for all manner of recreation elsewhere, never having discovered the *fullness* of pleasure available to them in their own bedroom. The Christian couple who have experienced this fullness will praise God together for what He has provided for them!

Fourth, the sexual relationship between husband and wife offers the unique opportunity to care for and be responsible for another human being in the most complete sense possible. Husband and wife are meant to love each other's bodies as if they were their own possessions. Not as mechanisms which can be used for satisfaction and discarded at will, but as treasure of great and lasting value. As we realize how infinitely we are appreciated by our mate, we develop the assurance of our own self-worth. C. S. Lewis observed that even his body "had such a different importance" because it was the body his wife loved! This caring and responsibility will extend outward to the homey details of life—paying the rent and keeping the house, buying groceries and cooking good meals, looking after each other all of the time. But it best begins with the sensitive appreciation of the other partner in the love relationship, and it continues to be nurtured there.

Inevitably we come to the matter of the mysterious oneness of the sexual relationship. To be two separate individuals, yet merged into one through a physical/spiritual act defies explanation. Yet we have the privilege of living it, of knowing completion through our marriage partner in the act of love.

"The human sexual union . . . leaps the walls of separation and loneliness, fuses our partialities and contrariness into wholeness, joins the fragments of life into a new, unifying identity," wrote George Cornell (Associated Press series, 1976). That this great completion takes place at a moment in time when we also experience the keenest ecstasy known to human beings makes it a miracle of God's provision to us.

And then it is so uniquely and amazingly personal—our very own experience which none can match or enter into. No one else can tell us just how to share this life with our mate. The dynamics are for each to explore, experience, and develop into a harmony as near perfection as possible. They will include spontaneity of life, freedom of expression, expectancy of pleasure, sensitivity in caring, and yieldedness leading to completion. But precisely how they will manifest themselves no one else can say. As you come to know yourself and your lover, you will know best how to love that special one. There will be "intimacy . . . tempered by lightness of touch, . . . partners . . . creating a pattern together, and being invisibly nourished by it," in Anne Morrow Lindbergh's words (*Gift From the Sea*). Your response of love, liking, and delight in each other will be as a bright thread of joy woven in the ordinary colors of daily life.

"Sex remains indefinable, inexplicable, mysterious," noted Cornell after writing a series of newspaper articles on it. "It's like a piece of Mozart music of which a listener once asked him to explain its meaning. Replied Mozart: 'If I could explain it in words, I wouldn't need music.' " So those who would understand the sexual relationship in marriage must experience it, and experience it the way it was intended to be—spontaneous, free, enjoyable, renewing, and more filled with meanings than words could ever tell.

11

Planning and Achieving Parenthood

"Lo, children are an heritage from the Lord; and the fruit of the womb is his reward," wrote the psalmist. "As arrows are in the hand of a mighty man, so are children of one's youth. Happy is the man who hath his quiver full of them" (Psalms 127:3–5).

Every child that is born should be considered as a real gift from God. It is my personal conviction that when both partners are knowledgeable and maturing Christians, they should have as many children as they feel they can properly train for a productive Christian life.

Husband and wife can know a special joy as they share together in the total preparation of their children for lives of individual service to God. Each child is launched out into the purpose of God as an arrow from their quiver.

God clearly pronounces blessings upon parenthood, but as many of you have discovered, parenthood involves giving, giving, and then giving again, without thought of receiving in turn. The rewards God promised come spontaneously and not on demand. This kind of unselfish, giving, and godly love for one's children implies that the parents are planning to rear them according to the Lord's instructions so clearly spelled out in the Bible. Parents who are emotionally mature in Jesus Christ will be free to love and give to their children without exacting something in return. It is those people who can expect all the joy and satisfaction God promised.

When I speak of giving, of course, I am not referring to a materialistic pampering of the child. A parent must give *himself*; he must be willing to invest all the patience and love and self-control he can imagine, and then some. Only those who give openly are open to receive—to receive the gentle trust of the little child; or the warm, appreciative respect of the young adult; or the tender moments of the growing years in between.

The Bible describes the godly family in Psalms 128:1–4: "Blessed is every one that feareth the Lord, that walketh in his ways. For thou shalt eat the labor of thine hands; happy shalt thou be, and it shall be well with thee. Thy wife shall be as a fruitful vine by the sides of thine house, thy children like olive plants round about thy table. Behold, that thus shall the man be blessed who feareth the Lord."

During the engagement period a couple should discuss their views on having and rearing a family and should be in harmony concerning the various issues involved before their wedding takes place. Their ideas may change later, but if they are growing together in their marriage, their views will take on a similar shape as God guides them.

This chapter is included to give information to those people who are considering the many aspects of family planning. One out of every eight couples in the United States is childless because of an infertility problem. Some have been trying to have a baby for one to eighteen years without success. Later in the chapter we will give some practical advice on methods a couple can use to increase their chances of achieving pregnancy. If there are no physical abnormalities, some simple procedures can more than double the chances of becoming pregnant.

Since seven out of eight couples do not have problems with infertility, the great majority of questions on family planning which a doctor is asked relate to methods which will control the number of pregnancies and the spacing of children.

Here are some factors to be considered:

1. A newly married couple need some time for adjustment to each other. It is desirable to have time to learn to communicate and to share before the responsibilities of a young family come upon them.

2. Fear of pregnancy may inhibit enjoyment of the sex relationship.

3. The health of the wife is an important issue. A woman can bear twenty to twenty-five children, and some have done so while retaining their health. But this would not be recommended for most women, nor desired by most.

4. Parents must be able to provide adequately for each child. But this does not mean that pregnancy should be postponed because of a desire for an unnecessarily high standard of living.

If a couple decide to postpone pregnancy, how do they find out which method is right for them? There is no method of contraception that is perfect for every couple all the time. A method which is satisfactory for one may not be suitable for another. Also couples may wish to change methods as circumstances change.

The first consideration obviously is *safety*. The best methods of preventing pregnancy must be as harmless as possible. Some methods are not suitable for women who have a past history of certain medical conditions or whose health is now less than perfect. Other women may find that a particular method causes them some degree of physical discomfort. In these cases your doctor should be the one to advise a method which he feels will be safe for you.

Because of the rapid advances in medical research and changes in government regulations, you may find that some of the information in this chapter may already need to be updated, particularly in the area of statistics and reported side effects. Before deciding to take any medication or to have any surgical operation for birth control, you must consult your own personal physician and depend entirely on his judgment and advice.

The second consideration is *effectiveness*, which depends in large part upon the user. Those couples who are careful to use a method properly and regularly will have far greater assurance of success than those who use it carelessly or irregularly.

The third consideration is the matter of *your own personal taste*. Any method which you find unpleasant, uncomfortable, or embarrassing, for whatever reason, will not be right for you.

I am not endorsing or recommending any particular method, but will describe from a medical point of view how and why certain techniques are able to control conception, and will list some of their advantages and disadvantages.

You may want to compare this statistic with those listed under each method: The probability of pregnancy from any one act of intercourse without any contraceptive method at all will be from 3 percent to 20 percent, depending on the time during the menstrual cycle that intercourse occurred.

Oral Contraceptives (OCs)—The Pill

The oral-contraceptive method calls for a woman to take a contraceptive pill or tablet every day for twenty-one days. A woman beginning to use this method takes the first pill five days after the start of her menstrual period. She then takes one pill every day until she has taken twenty-one pills. Then she stops taking the pills, and within two or three days her period should begin. Seven days after taking the last tablet, she begins taking the pill again for twenty-one days and repeats the cycle. This routine continues month after month for as long as the woman wishes to prevent pregnancy.

The pills are basically composed of two hormone substances closely resembling the natural hormones (called estrogen and progesterone) which are normally manufactured by the ovaries in the woman's body. When these substances are taken, they "signal" the body not to produce an egg (called an *ovum*). Since no egg is produced while the pills are being taken, no egg will be present in the woman's body to unite with the male sperm released during intercourse.

"The Pill" works primarily by imitating some of the normal body responses that take place during pregnancy. When a woman becomes pregnant, her body stops producing eggs until after the baby is born. When a woman takes the pills, much the same thing happens even though she is not really pregnant. When she stops taking the pills, ovulation begins again, much as it would after pregnancy.

It is important for you to know that as long as a woman is taking The Pill, it is The Pill that controls the timing of her menstrual cycle, not her own hormones. Since not every woman has the same response to a particular hormone dosage, there may be times when there will be some bleeding or spotting between menstrual periods. There may also be some increase or decrease in the amount and duration of menstrual bleeding, or a woman may completely skip periods at times. If you happen to be one who occasionally misses a period while taking The Pill, you must still continue your same scheduled dosage in order to be assured of protection against becoming pregnant.

Because The Pill now controls the timing of the woman's menstrual flow, you may be interested to know that a wife may, without any harm, occasionally delay the menstrual period by just continuing the pills a few extra days. She then stops taking the pills for seven days and then starts the twenty-one–day dosage sequence all over again. This delay of the period may be particularly desirable if the husband has a job which allows him to be at home at irregular but predictable times. There is no harm in occasional adjustment of these times of flow.

To regulate the time for onset of your menstrual period in this way, you must confirm from your doctor that you are taking the *combination pill*. This type of oral contraceptive has both estrogen and progesterone in each tablet.

Advantages of the Oral Contraceptives

1. When used properly, this is the most effective, reversible contraceptive method known.

2. No special preparations are necessary before intercourse. The woman is protected against the possibility of becoming pregnant at all times.

3. Since the pills are taken daily whether intercourse takes place or not, there is less temptation to take a chance on going without protection "just this once."

4. It is not necessary to insert anything into the vagina before or after intercourse.

5. No measuring or fitting must be done by a physician as with some other methods, such as the diaphragm.

6. Oral contraceptives tend to regulate a woman's menstrual cycle. Women whose periods are irregular may find this a distinct advantage.

7. If 1,000 women used oral contraceptives for 1 year, of these, only 1 would be expected to have an unplanned pregnancy.

Disadvantages of the Oral Contraceptives

1. Some women, when they first begin taking oral contraceptives, experience one or more minor discomforts similar to complaints women have in the early stages of pregnancy (nausea or morning sickness; spotting or bleeding between periods; gain or loss of weight; slight enlargement or tenderness of the breasts). Most women do not have these complaints, and among those who do, complaints generally last only a few days or rarely more than a few months.

2. Some women complain that they have trouble remembering to take a pill every day or that they sometimes cannot remember if they have taken it or not. It often helps to take the pill with some other part of the

daily routine such as brushing the teeth at night before retiring.

3. Oral contraceptives cannot be obtained without a doctor's prescription.

4. Doctors advise some women not to take oral contraceptives while breast-feeding an infant, as the added estrogens may decrease or stop the production of breast milk.

5. Every woman who uses The Pill should have a breast and pelvic examination and a Pap smear every year. However, this is good advice whether or not you are using The Pill.

6. There may be serious adverse reactions to any of the oral contraceptives. It is very important that you obtain from your physician a detailed list of possible complications each time you have your regular annual pelvic examination.

7. If any of the following conditions occur, the woman using The Pill should consult her physician: Frequent or persistent headaches; discoloration of the skin; unexplained pains in the chest; unusual swelling of the ankles; shortness of breath; disturbance in vision, such as "seeing double" or sudden partial or complete loss of sight; unusual, persistent, or unexplained pain in the legs; lumps or growths in the breast; frequent or persistent vaginal bleeding.

Vaginal Diaphragm With Spermicides

More than fifty years ago the vaginal diaphragm was developed as the first medically accepted contraceptive device. Used with a contraceptive cream or jelly, it is still a highly effective approach to contraception. The diaphragm is a strong but lightweight rubber cap about the size of a fruit-jar lid, from two to four inches in diameter. Its thin rim consists of a ring-shaped rubber-covered metal spring, which is flexible so that the whole diaphragm can be compressed and passed easily into the vagina. When released in the upper portion of the vagina it covers the cervix like a dome-shaped lid. The depth of the vagina determines the exact size of the diaphragm to be used. The doctor must measure the distance between the back wall of the vagina and the pubic bone in order to select the proper size of diaphragm. This measurement can be made by the doctor without discomfort during a routine pelvic examination.

Neither you nor your husband should be aware of its presence if the diaphragm fits properly. I would like to suggest that each wife who uses a diaphragm should prepare herself on any night when she thinks there is a possibility that she or her husband will desire intercourse. This not only lessens the distractions just before intercourse, but often arouses the husband's interest in sex when he knows his wife does not mind preparing for him. The diaphragm may be inserted up to four hours before intercourse.

Preventing sperm from entering the uterus, the diaphragm acts as a barrier or deflector. But to be effective it must be covered on the side next to the cervix with a spermicidal jelly or cream made for this purpose. If extra lubrication is needed during intercourse, choose a jelly. Otherwise, choose a cream. *I must emphatically warn you the diaphragm is almost useless without a spermicidal preparation which kills all sperm on contact.* The diaphragm must be left in place for at least six hours after each intercourse to allow time for the spermicide to work.

If you find no flaws in it, you may be able to use the same diaphragm for many years. You may wish to take your diaphragm to your doctor when you go in for your routine pelvic examination and have him determine if you still need the same size.

The diaphragm has no effect on future fertility and is a well-established, proved method which offers the security of the physical barrier in addition to the spermicide.

Advantages of the Diaphragm Method

1. The diaphragm and jelly do not need to be inserted just before intercourse, but may be inserted as much as four hours earlier.

2. When the diaphragm is properly positioned, neither the wife nor the husband should be aware of its presence.

3. Whether or not intercourse actually takes place, the diaphragm may safely be left in place for twenty-four hours or even longer. However, if intercourse takes place more than six hours after the diaphragm is inserted, an additional amount of contraceptive jelly or cream should be used. This additional cream or jelly may be inserted into the vagina with an applicator made for the purpose.

4. If properly cared for, the same diaphragm may be used for several years.

5. The diaphragm does not in any way interfere with sexual sensation.

6. If the couple desires to have intercourse during the woman's menstrual period, she may insert the diaphragm and have intercourse without any blood coming into the lower vagina. (It is not necessary to use the contraceptive cream if the diaphragm is used during the regular menstrual period.)

Disadvantages of the Diaphragm Method

1. Women choosing this method must first be measured and fitted by a physician. It is essential for a doctor to determine the proper size of diaphragm for each woman if this method is to be effective and comfortable.

2. The diaphragm must be used whenever intercourse takes place. Women who may not have anticipated having intercourse at a particular time sometimes complain that this method forces an interruption in order to insert the diaphragm.

3. Women who have a strong aversion to inserting the diaphragm into the vagina will obviously not be happy with this method.

4. If 1,000 women used the diaphragm method for one year approximately 26 would have unplanned pregnancies. This includes those who were careless and did not insert the diaphragm every time, those who failed to use the necessary contraceptive cream, and those who failed to use additional cream when having intercourse later.

The Vaginal Spermicide Method

These spermicidal products are used by themselves and are effective because they will kill sperm without harming delicate vaginal tissue. Available in three forms—foam, cream, and synthetic gel—these products are applied with a slim plastic vaginal applicator which automatically measures the proper dose. They are so effective that only one application is required before each sexual act. If a woman wishes to douche at all, she should wait at least six hours. Spermicides are significantly more effective than the rhythm, withdrawal, or douching methods.

Vaginal spermicides have been used for over forty years. The contraceptive action of these preparations is twofold. The spermicidal ingredients work to kill the male sperm. The foam, cream, or gel base provides a "barrier" over the cervix that helps prevent sperm from migrating into the womb. Many women have found this method to be safe, effective, and reliable.

Advantages of the Vaginal Spermicide Method

1. Vaginal spermicides can be bought without a prescription.
2. No fitting is necessary, such as that done before obtaining a diaphragm.
3. There is nothing to remove after intercourse.
4. Women who use this method need concern themselves with it only at those times when intercourse takes place.

Disadvantages of the Vaginal Spermicide Method

1. To be effective, vaginal spermicides must be placed in the vagina just before intercourse.
2. The applicator must be washed with soap and water after each use.
3. Occasionally a spermicide may cause an allergic irritation in the vagina.
4. A greater volume of vaginal discharge occurs following intercourse, as both semen and spermicide are discharged. Some women find this a bother.
5. If 1,000 women used the vaginal spermicide method for one year, approximately 76 of these would have unplanned pregnancies. This includes those women who failed to use the spermicide before each intercourse.

Intrauterine Device (IUD)

The IUD, or intrauterine device, is a soft, flexible, plastic loop or irregularly shaped disc which must be inserted by a physician. Uncoiling the device, he places it into a simple tube resembling a soda straw. This small straight tube is then inserted into the cervical canal and, by means of a slim plastic rod, the IUD is pushed into the uterine cavity, where it returns to its original coiled shape. This can be done with a minimum of discomfort.

There is some uncertainty as to exactly how the IUD works. It is generally recognized to be dependent upon the foreign-body reaction which is produced by its presence in the uterus. This probably hastens the passage of the egg through the tube and uterus, decreasing the chance for fertilization.

The question I am asked most frequently on birth control as a Christian physician is, Does the IUD produce an abortion of a two- or three-day-old pregnancy? My answer must be, I do not know. This question has never been completely answered medically or biblically. If you have an un-yielding opinion either way, I regret that I cannot give you information which might help you.

An estimated 10 percent of IUD's are expelled during the first year after insertion. Expulsion is more frequent among younger women, and is most likely to occur during the menstrual period.

Attached to the IUD is a firm nylon thread which protrudes from the cervix into the vagina about one inch. The woman can touch this thread to be certain that the IUD is in the proper place. Later, this thread is used to make removal of the IUD a simple matter.

A tampon may be used during menstrual periods. However, certain care should be taken each time the tampon is removed to be sure the thread attached to the IUD did not become entangled so that the IUD is pulled out along with the tampon.

If you decide you desire a pregnancy and would like to remove the IUD, your physician may suggest that you grasp the thread firmly and slowly pull out the IUD. There may be about one-half teaspoon of blood and perhaps some slight cramping. If there is resistance when you pull and the IUD does not come out, you will need to have it removed by your physician.

If a woman does get pregnant with an IUD in place, the pregnancy may proceed normally. To lessen the chance of infection, most obstetricians now recommend that an IUD be removed as soon as it is known that there is a pregnancy. If an IUD is left in place during pregnancy, it usually comes out by itself with the placenta (or afterbirth). There may be some cases when a physician will need to use surgical instruments to remove the IUD after the delivery of the baby.

Advantages of the IUD Method

1. Once the IUD has been inserted, little or no thought need be given to contraception by either the woman or her husband.

2. The IUD can be left in place for years without apparent harm.

3. After the initial cost of the IUD itself, and the medical fee for insertion, there are no additional expenses. (A medical checkup is advisable at least once a year, but this should be standard procedure for a woman whether she is using an IUD or not.)

4. Most women find the procedure for insertion relatively painless.

5. If 1,000 women used the IUD method for one year, approximately 19 of these would have unplanned pregnancies. This failure rate may be decreased even more by inserting a tampon a few minutes after intercourse. The tampon will absorb some of the vaginal secretions and semen. Since sperm can live only in a fluid medium, there will be a decrease in their life span.

Disadvantages of the IUD Method

1. A woman using this method should examine herself once every week to make certain the IUD is still in place. This is done by inserting the index or middle finger well into the vagina to feel for the short nylon thread protruding from the opening of the cervix.

2. About 10 percent of women are unable to retain the IUD because it is expelled from the uterus. We do not know why.

3. It is quite common for women using this method to have a heavy menstrual flow during the first and sometimes during the second period after the insertion of the IUD. The flow usually normalizes thereafter.

4. A small number of women may have some spotting or bleeding between periods, particularly during the first several months. This is most often a temporary reaction and has no serious aftereffects.

5. Some women, particularly those who have not had children, may complain of cramps and backache during the first few days after insertion. Usually these discomforts vanish within a week. Occasionally, however, they persist long enough for the woman to ask that the IUD be removed.

6. The insertion of the IUD must be performed by a physician.

7. Endometritis, an infection within the uterus, is more common when using an IUD.

The Rhythm Method

Three commonly known biological facts provide the scientific basis for the rhythm method:

1. A woman normally produces only one egg during each menstrual cycle.
2. This egg has an active life of only about twenty-four hours, and it is only during this twenty-four hours that it can be fertilized by the male sperm.
3. The male sperm is capable of living for only about forty-eight hours after it is released into the vagina. It is only during this two-day interval that it can fertilize the female egg.

The conclusion from these three facts is that there are really only three days each month when intercourse can lead to pregnancy: the two days before the female egg is released and the full day afterward. If a woman could avoid having intercourse during this time, then theoretically she would be in no danger of becoming pregnant. That is the idea behind the rhythm method. A woman using this method must refrain from having intercourse on the days when she can become pregnant. What makes this simple idea so difficult to put into practice, however, and what limits the effectiveness of this method, is that no certain way has yet been found to determine just which days are safe and which are not. It can be said generally that most women would be safe one week before their period, during their period, and for about five days after their period.

The success of the rhythm method depends on accurate prediction of the time when a woman is ovulating (releasing an egg). No *certain* system for predicting this has yet been devised. Ovulation usually takes place between twelve and sixteen days before the beginning of a woman's next menstrual flow, but the problem lies in knowing for sure when the next menstrual period will begin. The number of days between periods varies from one cycle to another and also varies at different times of a woman's life. Irregularity in the menstrual cycle is common among very young women and also in the years prior to menopause. Menstrual irregularity can also occur at any time when a woman experiences physical or emotional stress.

To use the rhythm (or calendar) method successfully, a woman must know just how much variation there is in the length of her own menstrual cycles. This requires that she keep a written record of her menstrual periods for eight to twelve months before she can rely on the system. Basically, this detailed record is kept in order to better predict the beginning date of the next menstrual bleeding, called Day 1 of the menstrual cycle. Once she has such a record, her physician can show her how to calculate the number of days each month during which intercourse must be avoided. Basically, she should subtract fourteen days from the next predicted date of onset of menstruation to find the day of ovulation. Then for the four days just before ovulation and for three days after it, she should avoid intercourse.

When using the rhythm method the time of ovulation can be predicted with greater accuracy by keeping a daily record of body temperature. This can be done with an ordinary fever thermometer but it is considerably easier to use a basal body-temperature thermometer, which is specially marked to measure even very slight variations in temperature between 96 degrees Fahrenheit and 100 degrees Fahrenheit. A woman using the basal thermometer takes her oral temperature as soon as she awakens in the morning *before getting out of bed*. It is best to take it at approximately the same hour each morning and to keep the thermometer in the mouth for a full five minutes by the clock. Generally a slight dip in temperature below a level that has been constant for a week or ten days provides a signal that ovulation has begun. This dip in temperature is usually followed by a rise of ½ to ¾ degree over a period of twenty-four to seventy-two hours. After two days of elevated temperature above the basal level it may be assumed that a safe period has begun. This careful written record of body temperature provides a check on the accuracy of the calendar record. It should not be used alone, however, because illness or activity may cause fluctuations in daily body temperature which have nothing to do with the time of ovulation. To be useful it is essential that daily temperature readings be made under the same conditions and at the same time every day.

A third method for determining the days of fertility involves observing the cervical mucus which at the time of ovulation appears as a lubricating vaginal discharge. The first symptom is a feeling of wetness more profuse than in the normal vaginal secretions. In some women it may continue to produce a watery sensation. But with many others, as ovulation approaches, the mucus produced by the cervix may become clear, almost transparent, and very slippery, like raw egg white.

At this point a woman can perform a simple test sometimes done in fertility-clinic laboratories. She may take a drop or two of the cervical mucus and place it on the flat side of the blade of a table knife. With the knife resting on a level surface, she should place the flat side of another table knife flat on top of the glob of mucus and carefully raise the top blade straight upward while keeping it level. In the stretch phenomenon known as *spinnbarkeit*, the mucus at the time of optimum fertility will cling to the upper knife and stretch upward like a thread to a length of four to eight inches. For practice one can try using a drop of raw egg white, but note that it stretches only about one inch.

The "ovulation method" of birth control is largely the product of clinical research by Drs. John and Lyn Billings, an Australian husband-and-wife team who stress the careful teaching of how to recognize the "mucus symptom," and they suggest a detailed record be kept of the cycle, whether it be a dry day, a mucus day, or a day of menstrual bleeding.

Caution should be observed in depending only on the cervical mucus test, as vaginal infections, intercourse, or douching will drastically change the consistency of the mucus. It is important to consider all these factors together rather than independently in attempting to pinpoint times of fertility: the day on the menstrual calendar, the basal body-temperature curve, and the consistency and stretchability of cervical mucus. When these factors are carefully determined and all three indicate it is the time of ovulation, then the couple can feel it is quite safe to have intercourse except for the four days before the precise time of ovulation and for three days after ovulation.

These calculations may seem to be tedious, time-consuming, and complicated. However, some couples have discovered a new togetherness in noting the intricacies of the wife's reproductive cycle and in planning and anticipating times for making love. This information may become extremely valuable when the couple is ready for parenthood and seeking the time of maximum fertility.

The development of a device to detect the precise time of ovulation has been announced by Dr. Harold J. Kosaky of the Harvard Medical School. The tamponlike, hand-held viscometer which more accurately measures the spinnbarkeit may become an effective aid to birth control or to determining time of fertility. It is reported that an inexpensive home version called the Ovutimer will soon be available.

Advantages of the Rhythm Method

1. No prescription is necessary. Nor is any sort of "fitting" required. (It is necessary, however, to seek guidance from a physician. Without it,

the chances of success with this method are apt to be slim.)

2. There is no expense involved other than the purchase of an inexpensive basal body-temperature thermometer.

3. It is not necessary to take pills or insert anything into the vagina.

4. There is no possibility of side effects or allergic reactions from contraceptive material. (It has been said that the only known side effect with the rhythm method is *pregnancy*.)

Disadvantages of the Rhythm Method

1. Success in accurate prediction of ovulation is uncertain in most cases.

2. The process of information-keeping for the rhythm system is complicated and requires accuracy.

3. This method restricts the total number of days in which a woman can safely have intercourse.

4. This method restricts the spontaneous choice of particular days on which intercourse may take place.

5. Not every woman can use this method. Approximately 15 percent of women menstruate with too much irregularity to use it at all.

6. This method is not recommended for any woman during the first few months after childbirth. It is usually considered unsafe to apply until after the third menstrual period following completion of a pregnancy.

7. If 1,000 women were using the rhythm method for one year, approximately 140 of them could expect to have unplanned pregnancies. This figure may seem high to some couples who have faithfully and successfully used the rhythm method. The figure, however, must be predicated on the same statistical base used to calculate the failure rates of other methods. This means the reported number of failures will include many couples who find that they were unable to abide always by the restriction from sexual intercourse for at least eight or more days centering around the day of ovulation each month. With total compliance this failure rate would be reduced to less than 30.

The Douche

The word *douche* comes from a French word meaning to gush or pour. It is a mistake to douche after intercourse in the hope of washing out sperm that have already been deposited—even if only minutes earlier.

Sperm are deposited at ejaculation in a forceful spray that lands at or slightly into the opening of the uterus. An average sperm travels an inch in eight minutes. Therefore, some sperm will probably have penetrated beyond the reach of the douche fluid. Furthermore, the pressure of the douche water may push some droplets of semen further into the cervix without harming the sperm.

It is not really necessary for anyone to douche at any time. The vagina is well supplied with glands and a surface which produces its own fluids which are sufficient to cleanse the vagina much as tears are designed to cleanse the eye.

Almost all odor from the female genital area comes from fluids which have dried on the outside of the vagina. So, thorough washing with soap and water is all that is needed to remove almost any odor. Additional cleansing can be done simply by cupping your hands and splashing clean water up into the vaginal opening several times.

The morning after intercourse, some women find the vaginal drainage of their own secretions mixed with their husband's semen to be uncomfortable. If this is a bother, they may sometimes wish to use a cleansing douche.

Here is the proper procedure for douching. You may use any one of several solutions: two tablespoons white vinegar to two quarts of water; or two teaspoons of salt to two quarts of water; just plain water; or one of the commercial preparations, following label directions.

The two main types of douching equipment are the bag (or fountain) and the bulb syringe. The bag type can be hung from a wall hook so that it is about two feet above hip level. Never hold the lips of the vulva together so that you put water into the vagina under pressure. Water can be forced up through the cervical opening and possibly out the Fallopian tubes, causing an inflammatory reaction which could become a severe pelvic infection.

The douche liquid should be at a comfortable temperature and should be allowed to flow in gently until the vagina feels slightly distended. Then, allow the fluid to gush out. Repeat this procedure until you use all of the two quarts of solution.

After each use, your douche equipment should be washed thoroughly with soap and water, rinsed, and dried. Do not allow it to touch a wall as it hangs to dry. Some vaginal infections come from candida (monilia) growing on damp bathroom walls. Your douche equipment should never be used by anyone else, and of course, it should never be used for enemas.

The decision to douche is a personal preference. In listing the advantages and disadvantages we will be dealing only with douching *as a form of birth control*.

Advantage of Douching

It is very inexpensive.

Disadvantages of Douching

1. The wife must get up immediately after intercourse to take a douche.
2. The wife loses the advantage of being able to relax and lie in bed after intercourse.
3. Some of the sperm may have already entered the uterus.
4. The pressure of the douche may push some semen further into the cervix without harming the sperm.
5. It has a very high rate of failure, almost the same as if no preventive had been used.

Tubal Ligation

A tubal ligation is a surgical operation performed by a doctor to prevent a woman from being able to become pregnant. This is done by cutting and tying off each of the two tubes that carry an egg from the ovary to the uterus. If the egg cannot get to the uterus and sperm cannot get to the egg, then there is no chance for the woman to become pregnant.

A tubal ligation must be performed in a hospital under anesthesia. There are three ways your doctor can perform a tubal ligation:

1. He can make an incision in the abdominal wall.
2. He can make an incision through the back of the vagina.
3. He can use a special instrument called the Laparoscope.

Many tubal ligations are now being done using the first method because the operation is performed within twenty-four hours after the birth of a baby.

The uterus is enlarged during pregnancy; therefore, the tubes are raised high in the abdomen, making it easier to reach the tubes within the first day after delivery. When a woman has a tubal ligation performed shortly after she has given birth to a baby, it is relatively easy for her and rarely prolongs her hospital stay more than a day or two. If the birth is by caesarean section, a tubal ligation takes only a few minutes more at the time of the caesarean section and does not prolong the hospital stay at all.

A description of the surgical operations for tubal ligation is given in the chapter "Understanding the Basics" in the section discussing the oviducts.

The tubal ligation has no physical effect other than to prevent pregnancy. There is no change in the woman's menstrual cycle, and personality and sexual responsiveness will be unchanged.

Vasectomy, which is sterilization surgery performed on the man, will be discussed later in this chapter. Because of its simplicity and lower cost, vasectomy is usually chosen by most couples who desire a permanent form of birth control. However, personal preferences sometimes favor tubal ligation, especially when it is to be done following the birth of a baby. It is important to remember that tubal ligation must be considered a permanent sterilization operation. A husband and wife should consider carefully before deciding on this type of operation. It is one of the most reliable techniques of birth control for the couple who feel that they do not want any more children under any circumstances.

Advantages of Tubal Ligation

1. There are no pills to take, therefore no medication side effects.

2. There is no need to interrupt lovemaking with preparations for the use of contraceptives.

3. Of each 1,000 women who have a tubal ligation, we could expect only about two of them to have an unplanned pregnancy.

Disadvantages of Tubal Ligation

1. Tubal ligation is considered a major operation and carries some operative risk.

2. There is always the initial risk of problems with bleeding, infection, or poor healing.

3. There is usually some pelvic discomfort for a few days, which generally is relieved with pain medication.

4. Only under rarest circumstances can a woman get pregnant again, if she later decides she wants to have another child.

5. The cost is usually from $500 to $1,000, less if done in conjunction with the birth of a baby.

Coitus Interruptus (Withdrawal Method)

Coitus interruptus means the withdrawal of the penis from the vagina just prior to ejaculation. This method attempts to prevent pregnancy by depositing the semen outside the genital tract.

There are differing views as to religious teachings on the subject of postponing or preventing pregnancy. We must say that the Bible is almost silent on this subject, and the references made to it cannot be used to form a very firm opinion either for or against birth control.

The only direct reference to birth control in the Bible is found in Genesis, Chapter 38, which refers to coitus interruptus or the withdrawal method. Chapter 38, verses 8 through 10 reads: "And Judah said unto Onan, Go in unto thy brother's wife and marry her, and raise up seed to thy brother. And Onan knew that the seed should not be his; and it came to pass, when he went in unto his brother's wife, that he spilled it on the ground lest that he should give seed to his brother. And the thing which he did displeased the Lord; wherefore he slew him also." We know that the Hebrew custom of that day dictated that if Onan fathered a child by Tamar, his dead brother's wife, the child would not legally have been his, but would have been considered to be the child of his brother. Even though Onan complied with the command to marry his brother's wife, he perverted the purpose of the marriage, which was to produce a child; he deliberately disobeyed the order given by his father, Judah, and therefore, he did not fulfill his spiritual and moral responsibility to his dead brother. It was not just the physical act but the spiritual disobedience which displeased the Lord. This disobedience required the most severe discipline God could give.

Requiring Onan to marry his brother's wife was apparently done for two reasons. First, to provide an offspring for the deceased brother and preserve his name and his memory, and to provide an heir for his property. The second reason was to serve the interest of the wife; otherwise, she would be destitute. It is safe to say that the brothers of the fellow considering marriage in that day would be most interested in who the bride was, since they themselves might inherit her as a wife!

Advantages of Coitus Interruptus

1. It involves no equipment or preparation before intercourse.
2. It is always available at no expense.

Disadvantages of Coitus Interruptus

1. The fluid that seeps from the erect penis before ejaculation often contains sperm cells. These sperm may cause pregnancy even though the ejaculation is done outside the vagina.
2. It is often difficult to control accurately the time of ejaculation. The discipline required for withdrawal before ejaculation may take away some of the enjoyment of the experience.
3. The sudden withdrawal may prevent the wife from being able to reach an orgasm in intercourse.
4. If 1,000 couples used the coitus interruptus method there would be only a 20 percent decrease in the number of pregnancies. This means there would be 160 to 200 unplanned pregnancies in the course of a year.

The Condom

The condom (also called a prophylactic, pro, sheath, or rubber) fits over the erect penis to receive the semen and keep any sperm from entering the vagina during ejaculation. Around the world the condom is still the most widely used effective birth-control measure. I have been asked why we hear so little about the condom as a form of birth control in this country. In an earlier era, laws were passed prohibiting the advertisement or open sale of condoms. Many of these laws remain, and this is unfortunate because use of the condom would also do much to prevent the spread of venereal diseases and even other annoying infections. The condom has been shown to be the most effective way of preventing the spread of venereal disease. Yet its use is virtually discouraged while governments spend hundreds of thousands of dollars unsuccessfully combating an increasing venereal disease epidemic.

Charles B. Arnold, M.D., of New York University has well stated the case for the condom in *Medical Aspects of Human Sexuality*, September 1975: "Comparative studies of contraceptive effectiveness have estimated that the condom provides protection exceeded in measurable quality only by The Pill and certain IUD's. It is probably as effective as the diaphragm. Thus, despite its humble appearance, its non-clinical sources, and its somewhat unsavory reputation as a method 'nice people' would not use, it is an important contraceptive method. It is, as well, the only one which doubles as a gonorrhea preventive.''

Here are a few simple instructions for using the condom successfully:

1. The condom must be put on before intercourse. Contact between the penis and the vaginal area should be avoided until the condom is fitted over the erect penis, because the initial fluid which seeps from the penis can contain sperm cells.

2. Allow one-half inch of space at the end of the penis as a reservoir where the semen can collect in the condom. Otherwise, the semen will provide so much lubrication to the shaft of the penis that the condom might slip off.

3. Continue to unroll the condom all the way to the base of the penis.

4. Very soon after ejaculation, while the penis is still erect, carefully and slowly withdraw it from the vagina. You should hold the condom in place at the base of the penis. (If the erection is first allowed to subside, the condom may slip off.)

5. If the condom should slip off during intercourse, grasp the open end of it and pull it out of the vagina with care so as not to lose the contents. Then the wife should douche immediately and lather externally with soap and water.

6. Each time intercourse is repeated, a clean condom must be used.

If a couple wishes to cut down on the expense of condoms, they may do so by purchasing a good grade of latex rubber condom, then reuse it many times. This is done by simply washing it thoroughly with soap and water, drying with a towel, then powdering it with talcum powder or corn starch and inspecting thoroughly by blowing it up like a balloon and holding it up to a light. If no flaws are seen, just slip the condom onto the first two fingers, and with these fingers spread apart, the condom may be rolled up just as it was originally.

There are animal-membrane condoms which are usually made from the intestine of sheep. These are a little more expensive and can usually be used only one time. Some men, however, feel that these afford a higher degree of sensitivity.

Advantages of the Condom

1. It is easy to use.

2. There are no side effects.

3. It can be purchased at any drugstore without a prescription.

4. It puts the responsibility on the husband, which some wives consider a distinct advantage.

5. Immediately after intercourse there is visible proof of its effectiveness.

6. It effectively prevents the spread of most diseases which are transmitted through intercourse.

Disadvantages of the Condom

1. It reduces sensation to the penis. However, this may be an advantage for some husbands who find that it helps to delay their ejaculation.

2. The condom can be put on only after the husband has an erection.

3. It interrupts sexual foreplay. This objection can be easily overcome by the wife lovingly placing the condom on her husband's penis as an additional erotic part of lovemaking.

4. The wife may experience some discomfort without lubrication. This can be solved by using lubricated condoms (hermetically sealed) or by using a contraceptive jelly which serves two purposes—lubrication and added safety. Never use Vaseline or cold cream, as petroleum-base products may damage the rubber in the condom.

5. There may be a small undetectable pinhole in the condom. It has been estimated that even a pinhole would contribute less than one in 200,000 chances for a pregnancy.

The failure rate of the condom when used alone is about 26 pregnancies per 1,000 couples per year. When the use of the condom is combined with the wife's use of a vaginal spermicide, the failure rate is less than 10 pregnancies per 1,000.

Vasectomy

The simplest, most effective permanent contraceptive method available is the vasectomy operation on the husband. This prevents the sperm from leaving the scrotum, thus producing sterility. The operation is usually performed in a doctor's office and requires only a small injection of local anesthetic to deaden a small area on the front and side of the scrotum. If a man has a desk job he can usually return to work the next day; men whose work requires physical exertion may need to take two or three days off. To prepare for this operation a man should shave the hair from the skin of the scrotum and have a good bath before going to the doctor's office. This advance preparation helps decrease the chance for infection.

A small tube called the vas deferens proceeds from the testicle upward to the seminal vesicles above and behind the prostate gland. This little tube, about the size of the lead in an ordinary pencil, can be felt by grasping the loose skin of the scrotum in the area between the testicle and the body and rolling the tube between thumb and fingers.

The doctor begins the operation by grasping this cordlike tube between his fingers and then catching a loop of the tube with a sharp grasping instrument. A small incision, about one-half inch, is made in the skin of the scrotum, and a loop of the tube (vas) is brought to the outside. (This skin incision is sometimes so small that it does not even require suturing after the operation.)

A section of the tube is then removed, varying from one-half inch up to two inches in length. An older man who is absolutely certain he will never want a future repair of the tube to attempt to become capable again of releasing sperm may ask his doctor to take out an extra-long section of vas. The length of the section of the vas which is removed determines more than any other single factor the success rate of the operation, for the longer the section removed, the less chance there is of a new channel developing. Even the best-performed operation can fail when a new channel develops through the scar tissue between the two cut ends. The failure rate for all vasectomies is about 2 per 1,000 men. Some husbands may wish to have a semen specimen checked every year or two to be sure of continuing sterility.

Couples should understand that there is a risk of incurring pregnancy for a short time after the vasectomy. The length of time until there is no risk of pregnancy varies. Time is not really the main factor, but the number of ejaculations is. Usually sterility (no sperm in the fluid ejaculated) occurs after ten to twelve ejaculations. Therefore, it is possible to be sterile in one week, but it may take as long as eight weeks. A couple should not depend on the vasectomy for contraception until at least one sperm-free specimen has been found. The semen specimen is obtained by masturbating into a small glass bottle and taking it within two hours to the physician's laboratory to be examined microscopically.

Probably the greatest misunderstanding about this operation is fear that it will adversely affect a man's sexual drive. The vasectomy does not change a man's sexual drive or his ability to perform. The tubes which have been cut have no other function than to transport the microscopically small sperm cells from the testicles. The fluid material that is ejaculated comes from the seminal vesicles and prostate gland, so that the amount of fluid released after the vasectomy is not visibly decreased. The physical sensations and enjoyment during orgasm will remain the same.

Occasional articles tell the reader that a vasectomy sterilization can be reversed, but I would advise any husband who is considering a vasectomy to regard it as an irreversible operation and not have it done until he and his wife have prayerfully decided that they will never again want to have children.

Advantages of Vasectomy

1. It is the simplest means of permanent sterilization for most couples who definitely want no more children.
2. A couple no longer has to be bothered with using other methods of contraception.
3. It is relatively painless and takes only a short time to perform.
4. The cost is approximately $100 to $300.

Disadvantage of Vasectomy

If a man should change his mind and desire to father another child, the chances of being able to reverse the surgery are very slim. The operation required is expensive, difficult, and often unsuccessful.

Abstinence

Abstinence cannot be recommended as a good practice in preventing pregnancy. This is the one method the Bible forbids. The passage in 1 Corinthians 7:3–5 tells us, "Let the husband render unto the wife her due; and likewise also, the wife unto the husband. The wife hath not power of her own body, but the husband; and likewise also the husband hath not power of his own body, but the wife. Defraud ye not one the other, except it be with consent for a time, that ye may give yourselves to fasting and prayer; and come together again, that Satan tempt you not for your incontinency."

Couples should strive to be sensitive and considerate of each other's sexual needs and desires, and to satisfy them regularly and lovingly.

Achieving Parenthood

Sex is intended for pleasure, and one of the sweetest pleasures comes as children are born. Young couples yearning for a family and failing to produce a child should find out why. There may be an infertility problem, and in at least a third of the cases this problem can be overcome.

Doctors define infertility as failure to conceive after one year of regular intercourse without the use of contraceptives. Infertility should not be confused with sterility, which is an absolute inability to reproduce. Infertility simply means the failure to achieve pregnancy within a specified period of time.

Studies have shown that two-thirds of pregnancies occur within three months of the initiation of unprotected intercourse. Within six months of such continued exposure, from 75 to 80 percent of women become pregnant, and by the end of one year from 80 to 90 percent have conceived.

The essentials of fertility are normal ovulation, unobstructed fallopian tubes, and normal semen. These factors must be present for pregnancy to occur:

1. The husband must be able to produce a normal number of healthy, motile (or mobile) sperm cells.

2. The sperm cells must be able to be discharged through the urethra during ejaculation.

3. These sperm cells must be deposited in the female so that they reach the cervix, penetrate the cervical mucus, and ascend through the uterus to the tube. This must occur at the proper time in the menstrual cycle for the ovum to become fertilized.

4. The wife must produce a normal, fertilizable ovum which must leave the ovary, enter the fallopian tube, and become fertilized.

5. Once conception has taken place the fertilized egg must begin to divide. After four days this tiny cluster of cells should drift down the fallopian tube and move into the uterus where it becomes implanted in a properly developed lining membrane and there undergoes normal development.

If a couple is unable to achieve pregnancy it is because there is a breakdown in one or more of these essential factors. Infertility is usually not the result of defects in only one partner but the result of several factors, often minor, in both partners. In seeking help both husband and wife should begin by having a complete physical examination, asking their doctor to search for any condition that might keep them from having a baby.

The physical examination of the wife includes a routine pelvic examination with special attention to fibroids, polycystic ovaries (ovaries which are enlarged), and vaginal and cervical infection. The hymen may even be intact, indicating that semen has never been deposited at the cervix.

It is possible that infectious organisms can produce substances that injure the husband's sperm as soon as the semen enters the vagina. The cervix of the uterus may be obstructed by thick or heavy mucus. Tumors in the uterus (fibroids) or an inflamed lining membrane could be the problem. An improper tilt or position of the uterus can be a barrier to the path of the sperm. The tube where ovum and sperm meet can be blocked by mucus or obstructed by scar tissue from an earlier infection. The ovum itself may not mature properly because of an endocrine disturbance.

Obviously, it is no simple matter to pinpoint the cause of infertility. In some instances, however, counsel and examination by one's own physician are all that is necessary. If the problem is more complex the couple may need to consult recommended specialists specifically interested in fertility—a urologist for the husband and a gynecologist for the wife. The couple may require repeated tests, observations, and treatment. Much energy, money, and time may be invested by the couple with no guarantee that a solution will be found. In the best fertility clinics a conception rate of 30 to 40 percent is considered quite good.

Although, traditionally, women have carried the burden of infertility, it is recognized today that men are causal in 30 percent of all infertility cases, and they are contributing factors in another 20 percent. The Bible recognizes the possibility of the barren male. "Thou shalt be blessed above all people; there shall not be male or female barren among you. . ." (Deuteronomy 7:14)! The husband is usually studied first in a clinic, since his evaluation is less time-consuming and less expensive.

During a routine physical examination of the husband any of these problems may be easily detected: undescended testicle, very small or atrophic testicle, varicocele, or prostatitis.

A testicle will not be able to produce sperm if it has not descended into the scrotum by the age of puberty. (Generally one should try to surgically correct an undescended testicle by the age of five years.)

A varicocele is any unusual dilation of the veins in the scrotum above the testicle. Ninety-nine percent of the time it appears only on the left side and is often detected only when the man is in a standing position. It is sometimes described as a "bag of worms" and is seen as a bluish irregular swelling above the testicle in the upper part of the scrotum. The condition is similar to varicose veins found in the legs.

Varicocele does not always produce infertility. Many men with varicocele have adequate fertility and normal semen quality. If a man with a varicocele has a decrease in his sperm count and a decrease in sperm mobility, significant improvement occurs 80 percent of the time when the varicocele is removed.

(*See* "Understanding the Basics" for explanation of prostatitis.)

Every man suspecting infertility should have a sperm count. Semen analysis is the single most valuable factor in evaluating male infertility and the obvious starting point. Since semen volume and sperm count vary with frequency of ejaculation, at least three specimens must be evaluated.

Semen is analyzed for sperm numbers, mobility, and shape and form as well as volume of seminal fluid. Sperm count is highly variable when different samples are taken from the same man. Normal sperm count varies from 20 to 60 million cells per cc (approximately one-quarter teaspoon). Yet there are men with sperm counts of less than 5 million who are fathers. Sperm mobility is estimated in terms of the speed of forward progression. Sperm shape and form is highly variable and a 100 percent normal sample is never seen. It is interesting to note that satisfactory mobility and the normal shape of the sperm are more important than the sperm count itself.

Postcoital tests are routine in an infertility study. The test is performed at the time of ovulation and involves microscopic examination of the cervical mucus a few hours after sexual intercourse. This allows a direct look at the moving sperm to determine how their mobility is affected by the cervical mucus.

Because most of the sperm are in the first three or four drops of semen, the technique of coital withdrawal may be effective when the male has a low sperm count. This is effected by a deep penetration of the penis as the first few drops of semen are released and then an immediate withdrawal from the vagina in order to place only the most concentrated semen at the mouth of the cervix.

Sometimes artificial insemination is recommended. Your physician places a freshly obtained specimen of the husband's semen at the mouth of the cervix on the expected day of ovulation. Again, the first three or four drops of fresh concentrated semen are used. This process should be repeated two or three times during the fertile period each month. Using artificial insemination for six consecutive months will result in conception for approximately 50 percent of normal (but infertile) couples.

Fertility is often influenced by one's general health. Trouble may stem from chronic infections, malnutrition, anemia, or various metabolic problems. Endocrine disturbances, particularly hypothyroidism and deficiencies in the hormones from the pituitary, adrenal, and reproductive glands can definitely affect fertility. The couple seeking a pregnancy should follow the basic rules of good health: Get adequate exercise and rest, avoid excessive emotional tensions, and eat a balanced diet. We know that vitamin A is necessary for maintenance of the production of the sperm. B complex vitamins are essential to pituitary function. Vitamin C (ascorbic acid) may be involved in preventing sperm destruction.

Here are some simple procedures to follow in having intercourse, developed by Dr. William H. Masters at the Reproductive Biology Research Foundation. These will greatly increase the chances of becoming pregnant if no physical abnormalities exist.

1. The wife is to lie on her back, her legs pulled back against her chest, with her hips upon two pillows.
2. The husband is to make the deepest possible penetration as he begins his ejaculation. Then he should stop all thrusting until ejaculation is finished and immediately withdraw the penis. Because 60 percent to 75 percent of the sperm are in the first three or four drops of semen, it is desirable to have this semen as undisturbed as possible. The acid vaginal secretions are unfavorable for the survival of sperm, but sperm survive well in cervical mucus.
3. The wife should stay for one hour in this position with hips elevated on the two pillows. She should then remove the pillows and remain for one more hour flat on her back.
4. The couple should have intercourse every thirty to thirty-six hours during the three days each month when she may be fertile. (Every

twenty-four hours is too often.) There is evidence that the egg must be fertilized within twenty-four hours of the time of ovulation. (See "Rhythm Method" in this chapter for an explanation of the use of the basal temperature thermometer and other means to determine the time of ovulation.)

5. There should be no intercourse for the three or four days before the calculated fertile period to allow the husband to accumulate the maximum number of sperm.
6. The husband has the maximum number of healthy sperm when he ejaculates regularly at least every four days. More than four days' abstinence will decrease the number of sperm.

If a doctor finds the wife's uterus is tipped backward (retroverted), a completely different intercourse position should be used. She should get on her hands and knees, then place her chest on the bed. The husband should insert the penis from the male-behind position. He should make the deepest possible penetration as he begins his ejaculation, then stop all thrusting until ejaculation is finished and immediately withdraw the penis. Though this will be a tiring position to maintain, the wife should remain in her knee-chest position for one hour after the husband's ejaculation. (Whether the wife achieves orgasm has no bearing on the probability of conception.)

The husband should avoid long hot baths if he wishes his wife to become pregnant. Very warm water slows the production of sperm by the testicles. In some primitive tribes the men sit in a cold stream before having intercourse as a fertility rite. (I do not mean by this to encourage any of you to sit in cold water!) Any tight-fitting clothing which raises the scrotum temperature to the same level as the man's body temperature for one month will usually decrease the sperm count enough to cause infertility. Loose-fitting clothing must then be worn for at least two weeks before a normal sperm count is again attained. Therefore, avoid jockey-type shorts if you wish to maintain maximum sperm production.

The wife should avoid the practice of douching, as the solution used may have undesirable spermicidal effect. Douching before intercourse for the purpose of cleanliness may change the normal acidity of the vagina so that normal sperm function and mobility are altered. She should make sure that no cream or jelly is used as a lubricant, because any artificial lubricant will interfere with the mobility of the sperm.

Any man with a low sperm count who is taking medication on a long-term basis should ask his doctor if that particular medication might be at fault. I refer particularly to certain cortisone drugs, anticancer drugs, antimalarial compounds, nitrofurantoins used to treat urinary infections, and certain drugs used in the treatment of depression.

There are several "fertility" drugs now being used to stimulate ovulation in the female. Recent research has provided information which is changing our treatment programs, and unanticipated side effects are being investigated. Please consult your own physician for the latest findings which may be applied in your situation.

Some practical things you as a couple can do to encourage fertility have been emphasized in this chapter. If you continue to have an infertility problem, ask your own doctor to direct you to a specialist with the required extensive laboratory facilities and a particular interest in this rapidly advancing area of medicine.

12

Sex Technique During Pregnancy

When the baby is on the way, questions arise: What about the wife's sexual desire during pregnancy? Is intercourse safe? What kind? When and for how long? Here are some answers to the questions most commonly asked.

There is little change in the wife's sexual desire during the first three months. However, there may be some discomfort during intercourse because the uterus is growing so rapidly. If this is the case, try the female-above position for intercourse. This will usually enable the wife to position herself for greatest comfort and pleasure.

From the third to the sixth month many women will function better sexually than at any other time of their lives up to that point. By this time most women are over their early discomfort and have adjusted well emotionally to the fact of pregnancy. They usually have a sense of well-being and may wish to increase their sexual activity. While any sexual arousal brings an increase in the blood flow to the pelvis which creates much of the eagerness for sexual release, the pregnant woman already has a great increase in pelvic blood supply and therefore will not require as much stimulation to reach the phase of increased excitement, ready for intercourse.

The enlarging of the abdomen usually does not interfere with intercourse in any way until about the fifth month. The couple may then choose to use different positions for intercourse which will afford more comfort for the wife. Here is a list of special positions, particularly useful during pregnancy, which you may want to try. Remember that intercourse in these positions must usually be accompanied by manual stimulation of the clitoris for the wife to achieve sexual release. Do not hesitate to add variations to meet your own special needs.

1. Husband and wife both lie on their sides facing each other. Intercourse is begun from the front. Or husband and wife both lie on their sides, knees flexed, facing the same direction, with intercourse begun from behind. This is usually very comfortable for both wife and husband and allows manual stimulation of the clitoris during intercourse.

2. The wife lies flat on her back with her knees slightly flexed or pulled up high enough to rest on her husband's shoulders. He remains in an upright kneeling position with his knees spread wide apart and her buttocks between his thighs. The penis is then gently inserted in the vagina. This position allows manual stimulation of the clitoris throughout intercourse and does not require any contact with the enlarged abdomen. The wife may be more comfortable with a pillow beneath her buttocks.

3. The husband sits comfortably in an armless chair with his wife sitting on his lap facing him, with a leg on each side of his body. This leaves his hands completely free for manual stimulation. The head of the penis may be placed just within the vaginal opening so that penetration is very shallow. This will be sufficient depth for mutual sexual stimulation and can be practiced even during the final weeks of pregnancy when deeper penetration may otherwise be prohibited.

4. In a position similar to that on an obstetrical delivery table, the woman lies on her back with her buttocks on the edge of a low bed, legs separated and knees flexed over the back of two straight chairs pushed against the bed, with pillows used for padding under the knees. The husband kneels on several cushions between the chairs, with his pelvis at the most convenient level for comfortable insertion of the penis. Obviously, this position requires prior preparation but it can provide maximum freedom and comfort for both partners at this special time. It offers excellent opportunity for manual stimulation of the wife and provides complete control of the depth of penetration of the penis.

5. The husband lies on his side across the center of the bed. In a cross position at right angles to him the wife lies on her back with both knees

flexed over his body as if she were sitting on his lap. The vaginal opening is placed as close as possible to the penis. The penis is inserted from below. The husband *must* use manual clitoral stimulation in this position in order to give his wife sexual release.

In the final three months of the pregnancy physical discomfort may diminish sexual desire, although in many cases it does not. With the baby's head well down into the pelvis, there may be a feeling of excessive pressure. For this reason it is sometimes better during the last month to avoid the female-above position, which encourages the deepest penetration of the penis.

Although some doctors prohibit sexual intercourse in the last few weeks of pregnancy, many others believe that the couple may enjoy sexual intercourse until the wife goes into labor if there is no pain, no bleeding, and no leakage of amniotic fluid. Of course, if for any reason your obstetrician says to abstain from intercourse during this time, you should follow his instructions precisely.

The question is asked: "If my doctor recommends that I avoid intercourse during pregnancy, is it all right if I reach an orgasm through manual stimulation?" The answer is that the orgasm rather than intercourse is usually the troublemaker. This is because, during the orgasm, the uterus contracts regularly and forcefully, very much as it does in labor. The habitual aborter (a woman who has lost three babies consecutively during the first three months of pregnancy) should avoid any kind of orgasm during the first five months of pregnancy. During the second three months of pregnancy, if the cervix becomes abnormally dilated, orgasm should also be avoided. Near the end of a normal pregnancy do not be surprised if labor begins a few minutes after experiencing orgasm. If your baby is overdue, achieving orgasm may be a very pleasant way to induce labor!

I encourage all of the Christian couples who come to me for obstetrical care to participate together in the birth of their child, with the husband accompanying his wife to the labor room and to the delivery room. In preparation for this, at each monthly visit to my office I have the husband actually examine his wife with me, and I share with him the information obtained. This allows both husband and wife to better understand the physical changes taking place during pregnancy. At this time I also give them an opportunity to share with me any problems which have arisen in their sexual adjustment.

About two months before time for delivery I encourage each couple to attend Prepared Childbirth Classes such as those teaching the Lamaze method of training for natural childbirth. Again, both husband and wife will benefit from learning together in preparation for delivery whether or not they choose natural childbirth. The wife may desire childbirth without any medication at all, or I may help her choose a method which will diminish her discomfort. There are a number of options which include any of the regional neurological blocks, inhalation anesthetics, or low dosages of Demerol and tranquilizers. If the couple is unable to enroll in a Prepared Childbirth Class, some help may be gained by reading *Six Practical Lessons for an Easier Childbirth* by Elizabeth Bing, R.P.T., or *Preparation for Childbirth* by Donna and Roger Ewy.

With the concerned, caring husband intimately involved in the entire process of pregnancy, labor, and delivery, there is a greater appreciation of his wife in her new role. She draws strength and encouragement from his participation, and their marriage relationship takes on new dimensions of maturity and unselfish love.

From the earliest days of pregnancy, the husband should keep this fact in mind: Many wives feel that they are unattractive during pregnancy. Their loss of self-esteem may become a problem, so it is especially important for the husband to be even more affectionate and complimentary than usual. Treating her with special tenderness and appreciation at this time will pay great dividends in sexual pleasure for both the husband and wife and will have lasting benefits throughout the marriage.

After the birth of the baby sexual intercourse may begin two weeks later, if sutures were not required. If sutures were needed to repair an episiotomy or other pelvic injury, you must get your doctor's advice on when to begin intercourse. Most repairs will be healed within one month.

When intercourse begins again, I suggest that the husband be as careful, loving, and gentle as he was during the first intercourse of the honeymoon. Be sure to have K-Y Jelly on hand. If there is no tenderness of the area near the clitoris, mutual manual stimulation to sexual release may be begun at any time after the delivery of the baby.

If the couple wishes to avoid another pregnancy, even if she is breast-feeding the baby and there are no menstrual periods, birth-control measures must be instituted at least by the time of the six-week checkup.

A word of advice to the wife: Remember that your husband is not pregnant. His sexual needs continue at the same level throughout the pregnancy, delivery, and the weeks of abstention afterward. You should offer manual stimulation to him at least as frequently as you were having intercourse prior to pregnancy. It is usually more stimulating if you use K-Y Jelly as a lubricant as you squeeze and stroke the penis to bring him to orgasm. Do not ask him if he wants this. Just lovingly initiate this stimulation and give him the opportunity to lovingly refuse if he chooses. Show your concern for him; let him know that you are longing to give him pleasure, whether or not you feel any desire or need for sexual play. If you then find that you desire to have your husband stimulate you to a climax too, clearly communicate this to him.

This period of concern, closeness, and consideration for each other can be one of the most fulfilling and meaningful times in your marriage. Many of you will discover that even in these special months, your times together are intended for pleasure.

13

Sex After 60 . . . 70 . . . 80 . . .

Sex after sixty can be better than ever! This is not propaganda to encourage the faltering, but a frank statement of fact. Many of my patients have told me that this is true in their experience. In my office a number of couples married forty-plus years have reported wonderful love relationships with more pleasure for both than ever before.

Now if this surprises the reader, it may be that you have been taken in by the myths surrounding oldsters. The myth of the decline and fall of sexuality by age sixty-five hangs on in spite of all research and information to the contrary. A cartoon published in *Punch* illustrates this false view of sexual incapacity. An old fellow on a park bench is eyeing a gorgeous young thing walking by while his elderly wife comments to another "little old lady": *"Albert has a wonderful memory, for his age. . . ."*

Let me assure you who are approaching the sixties or seventies that you will not have to settle for *memories* if you and your partner remain in reasonably good health and have a loving communication with each other. Attitude is the key factor. For instance, you probably look at life and the inevitability of aging in one of two ways. Some of you may think of life as a series of losses which must be adapted to. You therefore see sex after sixty as a succession of defeats, with the older person forced to give up more and more territory as the aging process moves in upon the pleasures of lovemaking. Others of you, however, recognize that life is a

181

series of changes, but you know that these changes may bring gain as well as loss. You find that as you gracefully adapt to changing conditions, you give up comparatively little while discovering unexpected treasures along the way. These positive-minded people are the ones who can expect to enjoy sex after sixty, seventy, or eighty.

Here are constructive suggestions for the after-sixty couple which can ensure a continuation or increase in their sexual pleasure:

1. Know the truth, and it will set you free!   I refer to truths concerning your own bodies and the effects of the natural aging process. To know is to understand and to overcome any difficulties which might arise. Here are some facts you should know:

First, if you have experienced good sexual functioning throughout your marriage, you should go into the mature years expecting pleasure to continue. Though some of the timing and frequency of response will change, sexual pleasure is far from over and may improve. Men and women always possess the power to bring creativity into their situation which will make sex after sixty rich, free, and full of surprises.

You men should understand that it will take more time for you to attain an erection. However, this can work to your advantage because you can maintain the phase of excitement for a longer period. Because your need to ejaculate is less urgent, you will have more time in which to give your wife full satisfaction. You can expect the ejaculation period itself to be shorter and the relaxation phase to end more quickly. More time (sometimes a day or two) will elapse between your climax and the ability to have another erection. Here is a very important thing to realize: *You do not need to ejaculate every time you have intercourse.* Never force an ejaculation when you feel no physical need for it. Forcing an ejaculation could diminish your powers to get and keep an erection. Ejaculate only when you feel like it. At other times, enjoy intercourse without it.

Wives, you should be aware that after fifty you have less lubrication, and the secretions are produced more slowly. This can be easily remedied by use of K-Y Jelly. The vaginal walls become thinner, less elastic, and more easily irritated by sexual intercourse. You can avoid the problem by taking estrogen or using a vaginal cream containing estrogen which is absorbed through the vaginal wall.

Although both men and women experience a shorter orgasm, lasting five or six seconds instead of ten or twelve, it still provides the same physical pleasure. If the wife should experience pain from the contraction of the uterus during orgasm, it is a sign usually that her estrogen levels are below normal. The condition is relieved by taking estrogens by mouth or by regular injections.

Men, the gradual, very slight physiological decline in sex drive with advancing years can be put in proper perspective by realizing that we reach the height of our sexual vigor at about seventeen or eighteen, and the decline begins then! The important thing to remember is that *aging itself will not prevent you from attaining or maintaining an erection*. You may ejaculate less frequently, less forcefully, and with less volume. But because sex is a natural lifetime function if you have an enthusiastic and willing partner, the gradual physiological decline will have little or no bearing on your sexual relationship.

Wives, you should know that women do not decline physiologically in their sex drive. In many cases women continue to increase in desire from the time of their youth into their seventies and beyond. In this period of your marriage you may find yourself becoming more and more active sexually, particularly with fear of pregnancy gone. Your enthusiastic participation will provide maximum pleasure for both your husband and yourself in the years after sixty.

Now I suggest that both of you check your attitude toward aging one more time. Remember, growing older is not synonymous with illness! It does not spell the end of sexual desire and pleasure. Impotence is not a natural development of old age, but is almost always a result of the state of mind at any age, affecting the man who worries about the normal changes taking place in his body, or who pictures himself "over the hill."

What then, you may ask, about the older couple whose sex life *is* declining? Several factors may be involved. First, not all individuals have a strong sex drive even in their younger years. Then some men become discouraged over the years because of continued rejection from their wives. Some, fearing impotence, protect their self-image by transferring sex drive into other channels such as the drive for financial power. Some men have developed resentments toward their wives which have diminished their sex drive. Many couples have allowed a set routine to dull the excitement of their time together. All these factors may be responsible for the decline of the sex drive in later life, but the causes are psychological rather than physical in most cases.

2. Decide to enjoy yourselves!   Understanding of your own physiology should be followed up by a decision with your partner to savor your times of lovemaking together and to let nothing interfere with this happy aspect of life. Know that pleasure is possible for you. Your love can be renewed, if necessary, by applying the principles discussed in chapter 3, "What If I'm Not in Love? How Do I Fall in Love?" More skillful sexual techniques as described in other chapters can inspire renewed interest. New, creative approaches to lovemaking can eliminate boredom and put the spark back in your relationship. The best "treatment" for a man whose desires are burning low is a warm, receptive wife who will offer plenty of loving sexual stimulation. (As the man said, there is a huge difference between being tolerated and being *wanted*.) Enthusiasm on the part of either partner can do wonders for the other one.

Here are some specific ways to find more pleasure in your sex life: Wife, encourage your husband by letting him know how much he pleases you. Husband, let your wife know how desirable she is to you. After sixty, men may worry about their lack of vigor, and women may fear rejection because of loss of youthful appearance. Loving, mutual appreciation will amazingly enhance your relationship and your total self-concept.

Be aware of what one writer has called the "background music" of the lovemaking experience. I refer to verbal lovemaking, which can richly increase your pleasure as both of you forget self-consciousness and freely give to each other in word as well as touch.

In touching each other, be sensitive to zones of the body which may not be physically stimulating but which may have a powerful and positive psychological effect upon your partner. Communicate with one another about this. Be willing to "adventure" in exploring new ways to please one another.

Discover the principle of *reciprocity* and let it work for you in increasing sexual excitement. Researchers have found that when two people are free of anxieties and inner conflicts, they can learn to thrill to each other's response and respond to the other's pleasure in a gathering momentum of delight, self-forgetfulness, and abandonment. On the other hand, rebuff, passive submission, or self-consciousness can have a snowballing negative effect, so agree with your partner to reject these influences. Life on this earth is too short to waste time in negative responses which hinder God-intended pleasure. Be on the lookout for them, and overcome them with loving communication and mutual understanding. Remember, communication means that you should never make your partner guess at how you are feeling or what you are thinking. Always aim for spontaneity and a relaxed approach to lovemaking . . . because it is fun!

3. Insist on your privacy. As couples grow older they sometimes find it difficult to maintain their privacy so that they can enjoy sex in comfortable seclusion. This problem is compounded by the insensitive or ignorant who do not realize that elderly people have sex lives. Your privacy with your mate is a priceless gift which should not be discarded except in a case of grave necessity. All people—but elderly couples more than any others—need the warmth and touching, the solace and reassurance of physical caring. If you go into some kind of nursing or retirement home, plan on an environment where you can live together with the privacy in which to express your love.

Although people with active sexual interests should not be restricted from living their normal lives, there are times when health problems do infringe and must be handled in a sensible manner so that the physical relationship can be resumed as soon as possible. The following discussion gives some suggestions for the couple after a heart attack, a stroke, or other physical limitation occurs. There also are important facts to be considered when the wife is going through menopause or has had a hysterectomy.

After a Heart Attack or Stroke

This, of course, is the age when such physical problems are most apt to occur. Adaptations are needed after a serious illness such as a heart attack or stroke, but if the patient has had good sexual functioning prior to the illness, most doctors feel that a return to his usual sexual life will help his total recovery. Often the frustration connected with sexual abstinence will use up more strength than would the sex act itself. The increased pulse rate, blood pressure, and respiratory rate reflect the emotional excitement of lovemaking, but emotional arousal from worry or arguing can have the same effect without the benefits of physical union between husband and wife who love each other.

A monitoring of heart rates of cardiac patients during sexual activity showed that the maximum heart rate response averaged 120 beats per minute and was sustained for only ten to fifteen seconds in most subjects.

(*See* ''Postcoronary Sexual Activity'' by John Naughton, M.D., in *Medical Aspects of Human Sexuality, 750 Questions Answered by 500 Authorities*, p. 124.) The activity turned out to be less demanding than driving a car through traffic or becoming angry. The energy required for sexual activity has been compared to that of climbing a flight of stairs or briskly walking two city blocks. Significant amounts of body energy are required for digestion after any eating or drinking. Therefore, I strongly recommend that the heart patient avoid having sexual intercourse for at least two hours after a big meal. It is interesting to note also that researchers point out that the sex act performed illicitly becomes a much more demanding function, as this combines the pressure of fear and guilt along with the physical activity.

For the loving married couple who normally come together without stress, manual stimulation to sexual release can usually be allowed after six weeks, and sexual intercourse may be resumed between the eighth and fourteenth week when the heart attack has healed without evidence of complications. This should be enjoyed in a leisurely manner with emphasis upon the pleasure of loving and touching each other. Although personal preferences should be considered, there is some slight advantage in using the female-above position if the man has been the patient. In this position the wife may be more protective and at the same time more aggressive in lovemaking during her husband's recuperation.

No specific restrictions are placed on sexual activity in patients with permanent pacemakers other than limiting of physical activity for the first two weeks. (*See* ''Sex After Pacemaker Implantation'' by Jorge C. Rios, M.D., in *Medical Aspects of Human Sexuality*, p. 126.) The personal physician must make the decision on an individual basis after that time.

We doctors should always deal frankly and wisely with the question of sex after a serious illness, rather than forcing the patient to ask or simply advising (ominously), ''You'd better watch it with sex.'' Sexual functioning is never improved by anxious self-watching, and neither is the patient's medical condition.

The aftereffects of a stroke often reduce a patient's confidence and sense of self-esteem. It is a tremendous boost to him to remain sexually desirable to his partner. Almost any physical difficulties can be overcome in loving, constructive, and common-sense ways, if the couple work together with the advice of their physician. Pillows, a handle on the headboard, a higher footboard, varying positions, and orgasm by manual stimulation are just some of the ways problems can be handled. A good sex relationship can be of inestimable value in coping with or preventing a patient's after-stroke depression.

Overcoming Physical Limitations

Strokes and heart attacks are only two of many physical conditions which may impose limitations upon a couple to prevent what we would think of as a normal sexual relationship. There are injuries, deformities, and the aftermath of necessary operations to be contended with. One of the most common disfiguring but not disabling operations is the mastectomy (removal of a breast). No couple should allow this operation to diminish their sex life in any way! It is particularly important for the husband to show his wife how much he loves her and how grateful he is that she is living and well. In every situation, two partners who love each other have opportunities to develop imaginative ways to provide full sexual satisfaction for each other even in what may seem to be the most adverse conditions. Learning these techniques together can become a powerful factor strengthening their total marriage relationship as husband and wife grow in mutual compassion and understanding. The goal should be for the two to live out their lives together in a wonderful closeness. As this goal is reached for, recovery possibilities are greatly increased. In every case the quality of the lives involved is unquestionably improved.

Occasionally a sudden, dramatic illness is followed by a period of total lack of sexual desire. This can be distressing to both husband and wife, and the reassurance of the physician is required at this point. The patient should be encouraged by the fact that this condition is almost always temporary and disappears when health is improved. It is most important that the couple continue sexual stimulation during the period after an illness, because loss of sexual functioning in the older person often follows long periods of abstinence for any reason.

Many men in the fifty-to-seventy age group develop enlargement of the prostate gland (benign prostatic hypertrophy). When this enlargement produces blockage of the flow of urine, an operation is required for removal of the prostate. After the operation the seminal fluid usually is ejaculated into the bladder rather than out through the penis. The ability to attain and keep an erection is not ordinarily affected by the prostate operation. The man will experience the same sexual drive and the same pleasure during orgasm as he did before the operation, but he should realize that no fluid will be projected from the penis at orgasm. Normal sexual intercourse can be resumed two months after this operation.

After the Menopause

Sex after the menopause can be just the same or better for the wife. Some women have had the notion that they will lose interest and pleasure in sex as they go on past the menopause, but this simply is not true. Changes in the timing of sexual response do not mean that sex is enjoyed less. Many women feel a greater freedom as they have fewer family responsibilities and more opportunity to develop their own identities outside of motherhood.

The woman who is experienced in love, who is comfortable with herself and well adjusted to her husband, can accept the physical changes as they come and continue to enjoy a rewarding sex life.

A minority of women may feel their feminine identity threatened by loss of the menstrual process and will make sometimes frantic efforts to regain beauty or sex appeal. A wise, loving husband will bolster his wife's self-esteem, showing appreciation for her in word and action. "Little things mean a lot," as the song goes, and particularly so at this critical time in a woman's life. Her husband may also encourage her to redirect her energies, perhaps into further education or into some Christian ministry. In fact, more and more retired couples are now going into missionary enterprises both at home and overseas to relieve overworked missionaries on the field.

Some women show definite signs of estrogen deficiency, experiencing hot flushes, nervousness, dizziness, insomnia, irritability, sudden mood swings, depression, and decreased sexual desire. When several of these symptoms are present, most doctors now feel that replacement estrogen should be administered either in oral tablets or by injection. In some patients the oral estrogen is apparently not well absorbed, and injections are required. A long-acting estrogen is usually given at monthly intervals. Most of the menopausal symptoms can be readily relieved by carefully regulated dosage of oral or injectable estrogen. Any woman who suffers from these symptoms should seek medical advice for a possible trial on estrogen-replacement therapy. If the estrogens alone do not increase a woman's sexual responsiveness, she may need some low dosage of male hormones (testosterone) injected along with the estrogen. Recent research has disclosed a very slightly increased risk of cancer of the uterus among women taking estrogens. Therefore, regular annual checkups are needed. Any vaginal bleeding after regular menstrual periods have ceased should be a signal to see the doctor.

After a Hysterectomy

The hysterectomy operation (the surgical removal of a woman's uterus) should not be a hazard for the couple's sex life. However, difficulties arise from a lack of understanding. Some of the common misconceptions are: (1) that a woman will invariably gain weight and lose her figure, (2) that aging will be more rapid, (3) that sexual desire and response will be diminished, (4) that she will immediately experience all the common postmenopausal symptoms. Sometimes the husband has the idea that his wife will no longer be interested in sex, or, disconcertingly, he treats her as though she were a china plate to be kept on the shelf. I have found it important to talk to the husband and wife ahead of time, dealing with any apprehensions concerning the surgery and aftermath, and assuring both that the only change may be an improvement, since most women having this operation have undergone discomforts which will now be alleviated.

Preparing for the Golden Years

I advise younger couples reading this chapter to prepare for their later years sexually as well as financially. ''Retirement'' will not mean retirement from the pleasures of lovemaking if you maintain an active sex life now and continue to do so. You should be making emotional investments in your relationship with your partner right now—maintaining open communication lines, living in an atmosphere of empathy and mutual support, practicing love for each other in all that you do and say. Every refusal to allow resentments or hurt feelings to come into your relationship now is an investment in future pleasure and a wonderful closeness which will continue throughout your life together. As you look forward to your later years, expect to love each other more and more. This has been the experience of many older couples who have overcome anxieties and inhibitions, have put new information into practice, and have learned how to please each other. They say, when asked, that their relationship is enhanced by a mature appreciation of each other and a love of greater depth than they knew as young people.

The maxim which applies best to sex after sixty is simply—*Use it or lose it*. The couple who keep active sexually can continue to enjoy lovemaking after sixty . . . seventy . . . eighty. . . .

14

Answers to Your Questions

Please explain why God apparently made the facts or techniques of sex so hidden that we have to be instructed in them.

This question was asked of me when I was speaking to pastors and marriage counselors at the Continental Congress on the Family held in St. Louis in 1975. My immediate reaction was that this is the most important question any Christian could ever ask on the subject. My response both then and now is that God has never hidden anything good from His children. If a couple carefully studies each section of the Bible which relates to sex in marriage, and if the couple shares with each other in open, loving, verbal and physical communication, this husband and wife will in time find the answers all by themselves. They will not need anyone to tell them about the techniques of sex. The Bible is open and frank about sex in marriage, and no man and wife who are free of abnormal inhibitions and openly communicating with each other need develop any sexual problems. However, people through the years have obscured the facts and principles which God laid out so plainly in the Bible, and as a result many couples need help in correcting faulty techniques and negative attitudes which may have been long established in their marriage. Newlyweds can benefit from learning the facts and techniques which provide effective means to develop emotional and physical satisfaction at the beginning of their marriage, so that problems are solved before they become stumbling blocks.

Why did God make men and women so different in length of time required for sexual arousal?

If men and women both were satisfied with a short period of arousal, the sex act would become a brief, mechanical experience. If both took a very long time to become aroused, the experience could become boring and monotonous. Some might not even bother. Because men and women are different, the husband is given the opportunity to learn self-control and encouraged to investigate and employ the imaginative techniques that please a woman. He has the opportunity to develop patience and gentleness in physical communication, while she learns to keep him sexually aroused and intrigued. The differences between men and women provide ground for creative, interesting interaction and enrich the sexual relationship in marriage.

How do I get rid of my inhibitions with my husband?

There should not be any shame in appearing before your husband without clothing, or in being nude in bed with him. You should feel totally free to do what pleases both of you in the privacy of your bedroom. Thousands of husbands and wives have benefited from listening together to my cassette tapes, *Sex Technique and Sex Problems in Marriage*. Hearing a physician discuss the intimacies of marriage encourages both of you to discuss sexual matters openly with each other. Have your husband read aloud to you the part of this book which deals with the subject of your particular inhibitions, and pray with him about these matters. The freedom to communicate your inhibitions to your husband in an open manner is one positive step toward being free of them altogether. Perhaps you and your husband should read together the seventh chapter of The Song of Solomon in a modern translation, to realize more fully the freedom that should be expressed in married love.

What advice can you offer to the couple who both work and find that any time they have alone is hampered by physical exhaustion?

This couple should be very careful to make special arrangements to retire at an early hour and may need to anticipate and regularly set aside quiet evenings to be alone at home together. I suggest an occasional weekend set aside for a brief and inexpensive vacation for two. The couple can make reservations at a motel in a nearby town for quiet relaxation and enjoyment of one another. If possible, a motel where meals are brought to the room should be chosen. There is little additional expense for this room service, and it adds just a little extra sense of luxury as well as allowing more private time together, which is the real purpose of the trip anyway.

How do you feel about the sexual counseling which encourages self-stimulation while the couple is making love? Is such self-pleasuring antithetical to God's plan for couples to pleasure each other?

I feel that self-stimulation in which the husband is also involved may play a very important part in helping a woman who has had a difficult time reaching a climax. Through this she may learn how to respond, experience orgasm, and establish correct response patterns. However, as soon as she is consistently able to reach a climax, the couple should resume regular sexual intercourse. Otherwise they may fall so into a pattern of just manual stimulation that she may be hindered in learning to enjoy orgasm during intercourse. God's plan is for each of the marriage partners to achieve full sexual satisfaction in intercourse. A man's sexual pleasure greatly increases when he knows he is able to satisfy his wife fully by bringing her to orgasm. Thus, the wife who *temporarily* stimulates herself as a part of lovemaking between the two (for learning purposes only) is not so much just pleasuring herself as learning to have a response which will also greatly please her husband. Researchers have found that about a third of women almost always require manual stimulation of the clitoris by their husbands in order to reach a climax, but this is usually done in association with the act of intercourse.

What do people do with the secretions that come out after intercourse?

Keep a small towel handy on the bedside table. A woman who finds that the flow of semen mixed with her own secretions is objectionable may even wish to wear a tampon for a few hours after intercourse.

What is the normal frequency of intercourse?

"Normal" is whatever is mutually satisfying to both of you. If you desire to have sexual intercourse every single night and both enjoy this and neither of you feel put upon, then this is normal. Five thousand couples were asked how often they had sex during a week. This total was divided by 5,000, and the average was two or three times per week. You will be able to raise your sexual desire to the level of your mate if you wish to, and if you commit this to God in prayer and yield your attitudes to Him. The secret is an enthusiastic involvement in the process of giving and receiving pleasure.

Is there any difference between a vaginal orgasm and a clitoral orgasm?

There is only one kind of orgasm whether it is produced with the penis in the vagina or by manual stimulation of the clitoris. The physical sensation is essentially the same. However, more emotional satisfaction is gained by the closeness and intimacy of the experience of orgasm during intercourse. Much pleasure comes from sensing the enjoyment of our mate as well as experiencing the orgasm itself.

Can a woman have more than one orgasm during intercourse?

A woman's body is designed to be multiorgasmic. If all the factors of love and consideration are present, and if the proper stimulation takes place, she can have as many orgasms as she wants. Hindrances to multiple orgasms would be inhibitions or lack of sufficient stimulation. The multiorgasmic woman almost always desires her husband to continue sexual contact and stimulation all through the time she is experiencing each orgasm. For maximum response she may occasionally request a brief pause in stimulation. The wife is the one to suggest the timing and intensity of the stimulation.

How long must a man wait after having intercourse to have another orgasm?

He must usually wait from several minutes to several hours before being able to have another ejaculation. The time interval of this recovery period has nothing to do with so-called masculinity. Keener enjoyment will result when the husband waits at least 24 hours after orgasm for the body to replenish the supply of seminal fluid. Often a man who is over fifty-five or sixty years of age will not be able to have another orgasm for about twenty-four hours.

Do you discuss oral stimulation with couples? Do you find any objection, scriptural or otherwise, to married couples demonstrating love for each other in this manner?

It has come to my attention on many occasions that couples early in their marriage have been unable to achieve sufficient stimulation for the young wife during sexual intercourse. Very often this is because the husband has been unable to sufficiently control the timing of his ejaculation. As a solution they turn to oral-genital sex to bring her to orgasm, and this becomes in a sense a shortcut, avoiding the development of the discipline and skillful control that is demanded in learning how to consistently provide a maximum of physical pleasure for both through regular intercourse. It is difficult for this couple to imagine that they are now shortchanging themselves, because they may both be consistently reaching sexual release, although without experiencing the unity and oneness that God has designed for their human bodies in basic sexual intercourse. I do not believe that God would have designed so many intricate details of the sexual anatomy to encourage husbands and wives to learn together the skills of bringing each other to fulfillment if He had not intended these to be used the greater part of the time. Also, oral-genital sex definitely limits the amount of loving verbal communication that husband and wife can have as they make love.

When a couple decides that sterilization is the best answer to their problem of birth control, which one should be sterilized—the husband or the wife?

The vasectomy operation performed on the husband is far simpler, safer, less painful, and less expensive.

Is it true that more men than women are being sterilized these days?

Figures released by the Association for Voluntary Sterilization, Inc., show that 639,000 men and 674,000 women were sterilized in 1975. In other words, more than half the total were women, who underwent hospital surgery as a permanent method of birth control. We can only assume that women are more keenly motivated to avoid conception than their husbands are.

What are the most popular contraceptives among married Americans?

Number one is The Pill (oral contraceptives). Runner-up is sterilization of husband or wife, according to the National Center for Health Statistics.

At what age may a woman stop using contraceptives without risk of pregnancy?

Menopause usually occurs by age 49, with a normal range of 40 to 55. It is estimated that pregnancies between 45 and 49 years occur in one to three instances per 1,000 births. After the age of 50, pregnancies are rare indeed, occurring in an estimated incidence of about one per 25,000 cases. Therefore, contraceptives can be safely stopped at age 50. When a woman is 48 years old or older and has not menstruated in six months, it is considered safe to stop contraceptive measures.

If I decide to have a child after I have taken birth-control pills for a period of time, will the pills affect my baby?

No, the medication will not affect the baby if the pregnancy occurs after the pills have been discontinued.

Does The Pill have any effect on menopause?

The use of The Pill will not delay menopause, but it may mask its onset. If the woman's age indicates that she is close to menopause, a specific way to make the diagnosis is to stop The Pill for six weeks and draw blood to measure the plasma FSH and LH. These gonadotropin levels can be determined by any physician by mailing the serum sample to any of several large commercial laboratories. An elevated FSH indicates that the patient is menopausal. If after stopping The Pill she develops menopausal symptoms, especially hot flushes, this gives additional evidence of menopause. If these findings are positive, the doctor can safely recommend that she stop taking The Pill.

Should a woman change her birth-control pill dosage as she gets older?

Since women over 40 on The Pill show an increasing risk of complications, it is often wise to minimize this risk by taking low-estrogen pills called "minipills" or "progestogen-only pills." With this type of pill there is a higher incidence of irregular vaginal bleeding and vaginal spotting. This may raise some false fear of cancer, but the spotting is usually caused by the pills. However, if there is spotting or irregular bleeding, one should have a pelvic examination at least every six months.

How does the size of a woman's breasts affect her sexual desires and abilities?

The breast continues to be the most exalted symbol of femininity, and the sight or feel of a woman's breasts is a stronger stimulus of male sexual desire than any other part of the body. In our bosom-conscious culture, women attach much significance to this part of their body, and they attempt to hide or display this area in accord with their attitudes, desires and goals, modesty, and discretion. Research figures indicate that only about 50 percent of wives gain sexual stimulation from the fondling of their breasts. There is an area surrounding the nipples which gives sexual arousal when very lightly and gently stroked with the hands or with the lips. In a few women this may even give intense sexual arousal, but other women do not care for it at all. The husband should find out whether or not breast play pleases his wife! Ask her.

Are there any disadvantages connected with having large breasts?

A series of medical symptoms may arise which are directly related to large breasts: fatigue, backache, poor posture, generalized numbness of the arms and especially of the palms of the hands, and painful chronic mastitis which may produce breast pain and tenderness. A woman with very large breasts must make a deliberate, conscious effort to stand with her back very straight, or she will later develop a typical modified hunchback shape to her upper back.

What do you think about breast-feeding?

God has a primary plan for the breasts to be used for perfect, trouble-free feeding of your new baby. We know too that the contour, consistency, and size of your breasts is better protected when you nurse your baby. Nursing also hastens the return of the uterus to its original size, usually within a month.

Can you get pregnant while you are nursing a baby?

Yes! While nursing may delay menstruation, it sometimes does not prevent ovulation (release of the egg by the ovary). Therefore, conception can sometimes occur before the first menstrual period after delivery. Women have been known to become pregnant as soon as six weeks after the birth of a baby. Some obstetricians even recommend that the new mother start taking birth-control pills before leaving the hospital.

How important is self-examination of the breasts? How often should it be done?

The screening for breast cancer by means of self-examination as well as physician's examination and mammography has increased detection of early breast cancer and has saved about one-third more lives of women who were found to have cancer. The self-examination should be carried out at the same time each month, preferably soon after menstruation. Women with a history of breast cancer in their families and those who have never breast-fed have a higher risk of cancer and should carry out the self-examination with great care. The procedure for breast self-examination (*see* pages 198, 199) was developed by the American Cancer Society, Inc., and is used by permission.

What causes mood fluctuations just before the menstrual period begins?

The emotional ups and downs that occur during the menstrual cycle, particularly in the four to five days prior to menstruation, are caused by changes in estrogen and progesterone levels. Probably at least half of all women who are having regular menstrual periods suffer from headaches, backaches, cramps, tension, irritability, or depression. However, only about 10 percent of all women suffer difficulties to a degree that their everyday activities have to be interrupted because of the premenstrual changes. Some doctors have found a simple way to explain what effect the hormones have upon the woman at this time. They equate *estrogen* (E) with *energy* and *progesterone* (P) with *peace*. In other words,

How to examine your breasts

This simple 3-step procedure could save your life by finding breast cancer early when it is most curable.

In the shower: **1**

Examine your breasts during bath or shower; hands glide easier over wet skin. Fingers flat, move gently over every part of each breast. Use right hand to examine left breast, left hand for right breast. Check for any lump, hard knot or thickening.

Before a mirror: **2**

Inspect your breasts with arms at your sides. Next, raise your arms high overhead. Look for any changes in contour of each breast, a swelling, dimpling of skin or changes in the nipple.

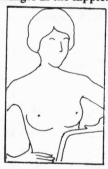

Then, rest palms on hips and press down firmly to flex your chest muscles. Left and right breast will not exactly match - few women's breasts do.

Regular inspection shows what is normal for you and will give you confidence in your examination.

Lying down: **3**

To examine your right breast, put a pillow or folded towel under your right shoulder. Place right hand behind your head - this distributes breast tissue more evenly on the chest. With left hand, fingers flat, press gently in small circular motions around an imaginary clock face. Begin at outermost top of your right breast for 12 o'clock, then move to 1 o'clock, and so on around the circle back to 12. A ridge of firm tissue in the lower curve of each breast is normal. Then move in an inch, toward the nipple, keep circling to examine each part of your breast, including nipple. This requires at least three more circles. Now slowly repeat procedure on your left breast with a pillow under your left shoulder and left hand behind head. Notice how your breast structure feels.

Finally, squeeze the nipple of each breast gently between thumb and index finger. Any discharge, clear or bloody, should be reported to your doctor immediately.

WHY YOU SHOULD EXAMINE YOUR BREASTS MONTHLY

Most breast cancers are first discovered by women themselves. Since breast cancers found early and treated promplty have excellent chances for cure, learning how to examine your breasts properly can help save your life. Use the simple 3-step breast self-examination (BSE) procedure shown here.

FOR THE BEST TIME TO EXAMINE YOUR BREASTS:

Follow the same procedure once a month about a week after your period, when breasts are usually not tender or swollen. After menopause, check breasts on the first day of each month. After hysterectomy, check your doctor or clinic for an appropriate time of the month. Doing BSE will give you monthly peace of mind and seeing your doctor once a year will reassure you there is nothing wrong.

WHAT YOU SHOULD DO IF YOU FIND A LUMP OR THICKENING

If a lump or dimple or discharge is discovered during BSE, it is important to see your doctor as soon as possible. Don't be frightened. Most breast lumps or changes are not cancer, but only your doctor can make the diagnosis.

women are more outgoing and active in the first half of the menstrual cycle when estrogen levels are higher. They gradually become more passive and sometimes depressed in the second half of the cycle when there is a rise in progesterone. Progesterone often calms the irritable nervousness experienced by women before their period when their estrogen levels are high.

What treatment is usually given for premenstrual problems?

Usually a mild tranquilizer is given, a diuretic if water retention poses difficulties, or an analgesic if there is pain. If these simple approaches are ineffective, hormonal agents may be evaluated. It may be found that an imbalance is present, with not enough progesterone to offset the estrogen in the last two weeks before the period. This can sometimes be prevented by giving progesterone tablets daily for about ten days before each period.

Is there any risk in taking progesterone?

Yes, there is a very slightly increased probability of venous blood clots, some increase in fluid retention, and the amount and duration of menstrual flow may be altered.

What is the place of erotic pictures and movies in increasing sexual desire?

Many couples do not understand what these erotic movies consist of. They show two or more nude people performing many different acts of sexual stimulation in extremely varied ways and positions. This would probably be offensive to most Christian couples seeking solutions in their own love relationship. Some psychiatrists who deal with sexual problems have said that they found these movies helpful in opening communication with patients and in sparking communication between husbands and wives who have been unable to talk to each other at all about sexual matters. These movies may lower sexual communication barriers, but viewing sex in this way is likely to produce more problems than it will solve.

Why do I keep on having vaginal discharge?

The three most common types of vaginal infection which may cause chronic or recurring discharge are trichomonas vaginitis, candida vaginitis, and nonspecific or bacterial vaginitis. The vaginal discharge which results from any one of these infections may result in painful intercourse, local irritation, swelling, or itching. Untreated, the vaginal infection may continue several months or several years.

Do these infections interfere with sexual intercourse?

Candidiasis (moniliasis), a vaginal fungal infection, is one of the few vaginal problems which may require a patient to avoid both intercourse and any other sexual stimulation for a few days at the beginning of treatment. Candidiasis frequently causes intense itching with redness and swelling of the vulva; often there is also a thick white curdlike discharge, and the extreme irritation of the tissues makes a short period of abstinence advisable. The discharge can usually be cleared up by inserting an antifungal vaginal cream or tablet high in the vagina daily for two weeks. For relief of pain in case of severe soreness, an icebag may be applied to the painful area for twenty minutes at a time several times a day. When candidiasis continues in pregnancy, the antifungal medication may be required throughout the pregnancy. This same candida fungus causes thrush in the mouth of infants.

How does one get candidiasis?

This fungus infection is commonly seen in a woman who uses unnecessary douching and vaginal deodorants or in someone with diabetes who is passing more than normal amounts of sugar in the urine. Candida is most apt to appear following a course of antibiotics or when there are elevated estrogen levels in the system: during pregnancy, just before menstrual periods, or when taking oral contraceptives. Nylon underpants, panty hose, and panty girdles retain extra moisture and warmth which provide perfect breeding conditions for fungi. Sitting around the pool in a wet bathing suit has the same effect. Cotton underpants are better-ventilated, and skirts are preferable to slacks when you suffer from this infection.

Is candidiasis contagious? Can my husband contract it from me?

Yes, he can. It will be seen as a rash on the penis or in the groin, as an itching reddened area with small round pimplelike places beyond the redness. Candida thrives in moist, dark places; therefore it is usually limited to the genital area. The man's treatment requires a bath twice daily to remove perspiration with thorough drying of the skin involved, then application of a prescription cream. He should wear cotton underwear and loose-fitting trousers during the treatment period. If this fungus infection lasts longer than two weeks after treatment begins, there should be a careful check for diabetes. The extra sugar in the tissue of the skin causes the candida to thrive, thus the infection is much more difficult to eradicate.

Which of the vaginal infections is most likely to become chronic?

The trichomonas infection is the most likely to become chronic. Symptoms include greenish or yellowish discharge with an objectionable odor, itching and redness, and some pain during intercourse. Because these symptoms are comparatively mild, the infection may be present for several months before treatment is requested. Trichomonas infection is transmitted from one person to another by way of toilet seats, bathtubs, towels, or any other physical means of transfer. This means that both partners should be treated, because the trichomonas can be harbored under the husband's foreskin or in his urethra and may not bother him at all. He may readily reinfect his wife even though she has been successfully treated. Therefore, condoms should be used for sexual intercourse during the treatment period.

What causes trichomonas vaginitis?

A tiny parasite which can be seen only through a microscope is the culprit. The trichomonads can be identified in a drop of vaginal secretion. At the present time, treatment consists of metronidazole (Flagyl) tablets given to both husband and wife three times daily for ten days. If the wife has repeated trichomonas infection, she may need to temporarily discontinue the use of vaginal tampons during menstrual periods. Trichomonas grows best in a more alkaline environment, and this environment is provided when vaginal tampons keep the blood (which is alkaline) in the vagina. This is the reason whatever treatment is prescribed must be continued, particularly during the menstrual period.

Are antibiotics the answer to these vaginal infections?

Actually, the taking of antibiotics probably causes many more vaginal infections than they will cure, because antibiotics kill the bacteria normally present in the vagina which combat a candida or trichomonas infection. However, some of the nonspecific bacterial vaginitis infections may be effectively treated by local application of special vaginal creams containing sulfa. Occasionally the wife may need to take antibiotics by mouth to completely eradicate the bacterial vaginal infection.

Why do so many teenage marriages not work out?

First, because teenagers in most cases cannot separate from their parents and become independent. Second, teenagers have changing value systems, and they do not yet know what they will want in a mate. Qualities later surface which were not apparent when the young people married. This is because character develops as a response to responsibility or adversity. There is no way of predicting with accuracy how a teenager will respond to the difficulties and demands of married life in the years ahead.

How much should a mother share with her daughter before marriage, using her own marriage as an example?

Much of this will depend upon the rapport mother and daughter have in all areas of their relationship. The mother should use judgment in how much detailed information her daughter really needs. No good information should be withheld once the date of marriage has been scheduled. The mother should see that her daughter has access to wholesome sex reference books. Hopefully the parents' marriage has been one in which husband and wife have been demonstrating all along a beautiful example of tenderness, fondness, and love for each other. If, on the other hand, there have been instances of sexual problems or indiscretions in the mother's own marriage, it would be best not to share these with a daughter, as this may damage the daughter's image of her own father or mother. The most important decisions our children make are in the years following the teens, and an excellent father-daughter relationship is more important then than at any other time.

Can diabetes cause impotence?

Yes, there are more than three million diabetic men in the United States, and about one-half of them have some degree of impotence from the disease. Diabetes decreases only the ability to achieve or keep an erection. It does not reduce the sexual desire, and in only 2 or 3 percent of diabetics is there any reduction in the ability to ejaculate.

Is there any hope of sexual fulfillment with a husband who is diabetic and having difficulties with impotence?

If the diabetic husband has experienced some problems with impotence, he will already have developed fears of performance. Many diabetic men can continue normal sexual intercourse if they will follow the procedures described in chapter 8 for overcoming impotence. Because the physical problem often caused by the diabetic condition is inability to have an erection, a loving, interested, and understanding wife can use her hands, preferably with a lubricant, to bring him to orgasm manually. He should use manual stimulation to give her sexual arousal and bring her to orgasm. Sexual fulfillment certainly is possible when the husband and wife care for each other and want to give the mate pleasure even though it is not possible to do this in intercourse.

Many people seem to think that elderly folk who are still interested in sex are abnormal. What do you think?

I think such an attitude is both erroneous and foolish. It is normal to have a continuing interest in sex throughout one's adult life. People should get rid of their myths about the elderly and let the elderly be themselves—ordinary people with sometimes an extra need for love and affection. The young will eventually learn that they have no exclusive rights to "love and marriage." Researchers have shown that normal interest in and capacity for sex continues into the eighties.

Do you have any suggestions for the pastor who wishes to give helpful instruction to couples who come to him for premarital counseling?

The need is great for more Christian premarriage counseling which presents both the necessary physical information and the biblical principles of marriage. Many pastors are now loaning a set of the "Sex Technique and Sex Problems in Marriage" teaching cassettes to each couple who comes to them for counsel before marriage. The pastors usually encourage the couple to wait until about two weeks before the wedding to listen to these tapes, and then ask that the cassettes be taken with them on their honeymoon to hear again when each is aware of more specific needs for professional instruction. For further information about these cassettes write to Scriptural Counsel, Inc., 130 Spring Street, Springdale, Arkansas 72764.

15

Your Marriage:

A Private Little Kingdom

Gaye and I have written *Intended for Pleasure* to help point the way to the sexual fulfillment every married couple can experience. Biblical principles . . . dynamics and techniques of lovemaking . . . problem-solving approaches—these all contribute to the total result. The sum of them, then, should be *fulfillment*.

But a cipher still is missing. Even if you have appropriated all the other material in this book, you will need this complete picture of God's plan for you and your mate. We speak now of your marriage viewed in a very special way. Look at it with us as a private little kingdom, a kingdom where you and your marriage partner dwell with the King, Jesus Christ, who is none other than the King of kings and Lord of lords!

What do we mean by a *private* little kingdom? That which is private is "removed from public view, secluded, not for common use." This is what marriage was designed to be from the beginning of time: a special world of belonging, apart from the rush and roar of life all about us, where we can always find renewal and refreshment in each other's love.

"Not alone . . . cleaving . . . one flesh. . . ." In phrases of rare and sensitive beauty, God's Word sketches the oneness and therefore the privacy of the marriage relationship. *Not for common use . . . secluded . . . removed from public view.* Does this describe your marriage right now? God has designed marriage to provide that which you as man and wife need to meet the onslaughts of life. But the Creator's design requires that you carefully maintain the principles of privacy and oneness in the physical, emotional, and spiritual aspects of your marriage.

The private kingdom of your marriage is not to be taken for granted, once established. Attacks upon your oneness will come, so be prepared. Look for open *invasion* from the pressures of the outside world—financial pressures, for example. You can think of others; they are easily seen. And yet sometimes they succeed in battering down the walls of our private little kingdom because we do not present a solid front to them.

The mode of attack may not be invasion, but *intrusion*. If we leave the gate open, intruders will walk right into our special private world where no one else belongs but the two of us and our King. Sometimes these intruders are family members, sometimes well-meaning or not so well-meaning friends or neighbors. They barge in. They encourage us to talk. They advise. They criticize. They divide. They cause us to see ourselves separately from our mate, and our kingdom is laid waste. We have lost our sense of oneness and all the blessings which go with it.

The most deadly and subtle of all attacks upon our marriage comes in the form of *infiltration*. We must learn to spot and unmask those most vicious enemies of our kingdom: heart attitudes of willfulness, pride, self-pity, resentment, anger, bitterness, jealousy. They slip in when we least expect it and bring desolation wherever we allow them to operate unchecked.

If all these attacks are successfully resisted and our private little kingdom of marriage flourishes behind God-erected walls, what will characterize that kingdom? What kind of marriage will we have?

First, there will be *security*. We will know a wonderful security in each other's love. This security begins with communication, and the sex relationship is a tender yet vibrant form of communication. Sharing, understanding, touching, pleasuring, satisfying the other in the safety of a committed love—this is security! Our hearts do safely trust in each other.

> To understand and be understood,
> to know, really know what
> another is thinking,
> to say what you will and
> be sure it is accepted as of value
> or sifted through without reproof
> to be you, really *you*,
> and know you are loved—
> This is near-heaven.
>
> GLORIA OKES PERKINS

Our physical love relationship becomes the walled garden, the inner courtyard of the kingdom, and it is a sacred place. We trust that by now, if not before, you have the biblical perspective of the sacredness of sex in marriage so firmly implanted in your understanding that you and your mate will be able to grow in joy and to increase in pleasure from year to year as God intended.

Please remember how very important it is to make the act of love a central part of your life. In other words, schedule time for each other. Plan your evenings so that you have nights when you can be alone together to enjoy each other fully, without weariness or interruption. Plan an occasional private weekend trip just for the two of you.

Second, there will be *stability*. We will appreciate a blessed stability in the order of our home if it is established on God-defined lines. We each will know our positions, our responsibilities, our rights. We will not be hampered or shaken by fluctuating relationships resulting from continually shifting roles. When we enjoy the stability that order brings, we will find freedom for growth such as we could never know in a fluid situation.

This stability that comes when marriage, home, and family are operated according to God's order can become a powerful safety measure, keeping your kingdom at peace. This means that your marriage will not be a patriarchy where husband rules as a dictator. Nor a matriarchy where wife rules as the awesome power behind the throne. It will not be an anarchy where no one has answered the question "Who's in charge?" (When there are no rules, children usually end up in control, and this is the most destructive government of all.) Instead, your marriage will be a theocracy, where God rules—where the husband is the head of the house because he is responsible to carry out the will of God; where the wife operates under the covering of her husband's love, wisdom, and protection; where the children obey their parents. "But I would have you know that the head of every man is Christ; and the head of the woman is the man; and the head of Christ is God" (1 Corinthians 11:3).

Third, there will be *serenity*. A private little kingdom operating under the truths of the Word of God surely will have serenity as the very air of the land. Serenity flows from a harmony of beliefs, a oneness of goals, a mutual participation in all that is most important to the man and the wife. Since God is never the author of confusion, serenity will exist wherever God is in control.

Centuries ago, the poet Omar Khayyám wrote:

Ah, Love! could you and I with Fate
conspire
To grasp this sorry Scheme of Things
entire,
Would not we shatter it to bits—and
then
Re-mould it nearer to the Heart's Desire!

We have counseled with many couples whose hearts said the same thing. They longed to start all over again with each other, their mistakes of the past and their wrong ways of doing things shattered in an instant, so that they could reshape their marriage nearer to the heart's desire.

It *is* possible for you to do this. You can change your world, the world of your marriage, if it is not now the private kingdom of God's design. It *can* be the intimate, precious relationship of total commitment that it was always meant to be.

The resources for this change come from the power of God as made available to you in the Lord Jesus Christ. He can enable you to love and give, to forgive and ask forgiveness, to forget yourself in your caring for your loved one, and, in turn, to receive joyfully from your mate. He can make it possible for you to see when a conflict arises that the real problem is *you*. As you act on the basis of your responsibilities rather than clinging to your rights, the conflict will resolve itself with an even stronger welding of the two of you into one. He can cause you to be sensitive to each other's needs, always ''on the other's team,'' always seeing that which is admirable in the other, and never focusing on faults and failures. He will make your marriage ever more intimate and harmonious and full of delights.

This truly is a world nearer to the heart's desire, isn't it? But it requires a King for your private little kingdom, a King who can empower you to bring it into being.

That King is the Lord Jesus Christ, who at a specific moment in history died on the cross and bore the sins of the whole world. Through that mighty act, He opened the way for all our sins to be forgiven, for the death penalty had already been paid. In Jesus our past is not only pardoned but our sins forgotten as if they were put in the bottom of the deepest ocean and remembered no more. After three days in the grave, to demonstrate to all people for all time that He is God, Jesus arose again from the dead with all power and authority and resources for the life of the one who believes on Him. It is written, "For as many as received Him, to them gave He the power to become the sons of God, even to them that believe on His name" (John 1:12).

If you have not asked Jesus to be your Saviour you can do it now. It can be done as simply as the man healed of blindness in John 9:35–38. "Jesus . . . said unto him, Dost thou believe on the Son of God? He answered, and said, Who is He, Lord, that I might believe on Him? And Jesus said unto him, Thou hast both seen Him, and it is He that talketh with thee. And he said, Lord, I believe. And he worshiped Him."

Or here is a prayer which you may offer to express your faith in Jesus Christ as your Saviour:

> Dear Heavenly Father, I realize I am a sinner and cannot do one thing to save myself. Right now I believe Jesus Christ died on the cross, shedding His blood as full payment for my sins—past, present, and future—and by rising from the dead demonstrated that He is God.
>
> As best I know how, I am believing in Him, putting all my trust in Jesus Christ as my personal Saviour, as my only hope for salvation and eternal life.
>
> Right now I am receiving Christ into my life and I thank You for saving me as You promised, and I ask that You will give me increasing faith and wisdom as I study and believe Your Word.
>
> For I ask this in Christ's name. Amen.

Gaye and I would like to hear from you if you have just now trusted Christ. Our prayer for each reader is that you and your partner will be guided into that oneness which will cause the love in your marriage to reveal to the world the image of the union between Christ and His Church.

> For this cause shall a man leave his father and mother, and shall be joined unto his wife, and they two shall be one flesh. This is a great mystery, but I speak concerning Christ and the church. Nevertheless, let every one of you in particular so love his wife even as himself; and the wife, see that she reverence her husband.
>
> Ephesians 5:31–33

Suggested Reading

Berry, Jo. *Happy Home Handbook*. Old Tappan, New Jersey: Fleming H. Revell Company, 1976. (An excellent workbook presenting woman's place in the home.)

Bright, Vonette Z. *For Such a Time as This*. Old Tappan, New Jersey: Fleming H. Revell Company, 1976. (Gives practical advice based on her experience in revitalizing her full potential as a wife, mother, homemaker, and as a committed Christian.)

Cooper, Darien B. *You Can Be the Wife of a Happy Husband*. Wheaton, Illinois: SP Publications Inc., Victor Books, 1974. (Develops the wife's God-given role on a practical level.)

Dobson, James. *What Wives Wish Their Husbands Knew About Women*. Wheaton, Illinois: Tyndale House Publishers, Inc., 1975. (Includes an important section on hormonal problems during menopause.)

Guernsey, Dennis. *Thoroughly Married*. Waco, Texas: Word Books, 1976. (A refreshing, concise, yet thorough treatment of the most delicate problems within the marriage relationship.)

Hendricks, Howard G. *Christian Counseling for Contemporary Problems*. 3d ed. Dallas: Christian Educational Department, Dallas Theological Seminary, 1968. (Gives a rather complete outline of counseling procedures for common problems. This should be invaluable for any Christian counselor.)

LaHaye, Tim and Beverly. *The Act of Marriage: The Beauty of Sexual Love*. Grand Rapids, Michigan: Zondervan Publishing House, 1976. (A beautiful presentation which offers practical suggestions for improving the sex relationship in any marriage.)

————. *How to Be Happy Though Married*. Wheaton, Illinois: Tyndale House Publishers, Inc., 1968. (Helpful in establishing healthy attitudes in marriage.)

Landorf, Joyce. *Tough and Tender*. Old Tappan, New Jersey: Fleming H. Revell Company, 1975. (A sensitive portrayal of the husband and wife roles in marriage.)

Miles, Herbert J. *Sexual Happiness in Marriage*. Grand Rapids, Michigan: Zondervan Publishing House, 1967. (A classic, written by one who has pioneered in presenting sex and marriage from the Biblical viewpoint.)

————. *Sexual Understanding Before Marriage*. Grand Rapids, Michigan: Zondervan Publishing House, 1971. (A guide for the young adult in facing sexual pressures. Also helpful for counselors who work with teens.)

————. *The Dating Game*. Grand Rapids, Michigan: Zondervan Publishing House, 1971. (A valuable discussion of the many facets of courtship with specific helps in planning the honeymoon.)

Minirth, Frank B. (M.D.) *Christian Psychiatry*. Old Tappan, New Jersey: Fleming H. Revell Company, 1977. (A sound approach to personal problems which may interfere with development of good relationships in marriage.)

Morgan, Marabel. *The Total Woman*. Old Tappan, New Jersey: Fleming H. Revell Company, 1973. (Gives practical advice based on her experience in revitalizing her marriage.)

―――. *Total Joy*. Old Tappan, New Jersey: Fleming H. Revell Company, 1976. (Tells how today's woman can find personal joy and contentment by living according to Bible truths.)

Painter, Alice. *The Challenge of Being a Woman*. Bible Believers Book and Supply Center, Inc., 130 Spring St., Springdale, Arkansas 72764, 1976 (A fine workbook study from the woman's view. Accompanying tapes are also available.)

Petersen, J. Allan. *The Marriage Affair*. Wheaton, Illinois: Tyndale House Publishers, Inc., 1971. (Valuable information on marriage—a composite picture.)

―――. *For Men Only*. Wheaton, Illinois: Tyndale House Publishers, 1973.

―――. *Two Become One*. Wheaton, Illinois: Tyndale House Publishers, 1973.

Rice, Shirley. *Physical Unity in Marriage*. The Tabernacle Church of Norfolk, 7120 Granby St., Norfolk, Virginia, 1973. (Outstanding treatment of the subject—a woman's book.)

―――. *The Christian Home: A Woman's View*. The Tabernacle Church of Norfolk, 7120 Granby St., Norfolk, Virginia, 1965.

Roberts, Douglas. *To Adam with Love*. Old Tappan, New Jersey: Fleming H. Revell Company, Spire Books, 1974. (Concise overview of the marriage relationship.)

Sanchez, George. *Scriptural Home Seminar Workbook*. Colorado Springs, Colorado: The Navigators, 1973. (An excellent study tool for husband and wife. Cassettes accompany the workbook.)

Timmons, Tim. *Maximum Marriage*. Old Tappan, New Jersey: Fleming H. Revell Company, 1976. (Practical advice in resolving conflicts and establishing desirable attitudes.)

Wright, H. Norman. *Communication: Key to Your Marriage*. Glendale, California: G/L Publications, 1974. (Ideas which can lead couples into more effective communication patterns.)

Reading for the Counselor or Physician

Clark, LeMon, M.D. *The Enjoyment of Love in Marriage*. New York: The New American Library, Inc. Signet Books, 1969.

Hartman, William E., and Fithian, Marilyn A. *Treatment of Sexual Dysfunction*. Long Beach, California: Center for Marital and Sexual Studies, 1972.

Kaplan, Helen Singer, M.D. *The New Sex Therapy*. New York: The New York Times Book Company, 1974.

Masters, William H., and Johnson, Virginia E. *Human Sexual Response*. Boston: Little, Brown & Co., 1966.

————— *Human Sexual Inadequacy*. Boston: Little, Brown & Co., 1970.

Minirth, Frank B. (M.D.) *Christian Psychiatry*. Old Tappan, New Jersey: Fleming H. Revell Company, 1977. (A sound approach to personal problems which may interfere with development of good relationships in marriage.)

Index

215